GROWTH THROUGH ENGLISH

D1355705

Growth through English

English

SET IN THE PERSPECTIVE OF THE SEVENTIES

John Dixon

Published for the
NATIONAL ASSOCIATION FOR THE
TEACHING OF ENGLISH
by the Oxford University Press

9523

This book is published for the National Association for the Teaching of English (Great Britain) on behalf of the Association; The National Council of Teachers of English, 1111 Kenyon Road, Urbana, Illinois; 61801; and the Modern Language Association, 6 Washington Square N. New York 3.

© JOHN DIXON 1967, 1969, 1975

First published 1967
Second edition 1969
Reprinted 1970, 1971, 1972
Third Edition 1975

Printed in Great Britain by
Cox & Wyman Ltd., London, Reading and Fakenham

NATIONAL ASSOCIATION FOR THE TEACHING OF ENGLISH
5 Imperial Road, Edgerton, Huddersfield, Yorkshire.

Contents

Foreword

WE must begin by recognizing the honour conferred upon us by the author, publishers, and sponsoring organizations in inviting us to write the introduction to a revised edition of *Growth through English*. It is unlikely that any other book in the past decade has had more influence upon English work in classrooms on both sides of the Atlantic, and we share the hope that this new edition may give that influence renewed impetus.

As we set out on our task, we cannot help recalling the last occasion on which we sat down to draft a joint paper. It was on a Sunday evening in Dartmouth—the return to work after a brief respite from the pressures of that hard-working month. Most of us had spent the weekend in the sunshine, exploring the New England countryside. The topic of that paper, "Process, Knowledge, and the English Programme", made it a rather formidable return. If having the Atlantic between us does not discourage us from attempting a joint draft today, we owe it to the opportunities for interaction that resulted directly from the Dartmouth Seminar—an interaction that has become steadily more widespread among the members of N.C.T.E., the M.L.A., C.C.T.E. and N.A.T.E., and in recent months has also drawn in representatives of the Australian Association for the Teaching of English.

We grow more and more convinced that effective curriculum change begins with a teacher reflecting upon his own experience. New knowledge, hypotheses derived from research and scholarship, new theories about learning are valuable in this context in so far as teachers are able to draw upon them in considering their own experience and thereafter modifying their classroom behaviour. Guidelines and syllabuses that reflect new knowledge form a helpful background to a teacher's activities, but they exist only as options he *may* take up; how and why he takes them up will determine the outcomes in practice. Put very simply, we must accept that innovation will be sporadic at first, move into clusters, become a network, and gradually gain increasing prevalence and recognition. In such a progression it will be clear that books are important—only less important, in fact, than face-to-face talk among teachers; guidelines, pronouncements, and manifestos come lower down on the list.

Changes in the nature of and support for research and development 1966–74

We cannot reflect upon what has happened to the ideas expressed at Dartmouth and interpreted in *Growth through English* without commenting on the climate for curricular change that existed in both of our countries during that summer and the dramatic, often traumatic changes of the past decade which have at times influenced individual interpretation of John Dixon's work.

The issue at Dartmouth in 1966 was curriculum development. Americans, coming directly from four years of federally-supported curriculum development known as *Project English*, hoped to share their experience with colleagues from the U.K. and Canada. Federally supported summer institutes had provided new perspectives on the content of English courses to thirteen and a half thousand American teachers of English. Great national foundations seemed willing to provide funds for worthwhile educational projects (as the Carnegie Corporation of New York supported the conference in Hanover). No American seriously questioned that this largesse would continue, and if some American participants confidently expected a "blueprint" for future research and development to emerge from Dartmouth, their optimism can at least be understood.

For the English delegates, with far less in the way of "projects" to look back on, but with the green light of the newly-formed Schools Council shining in their eyes—and dazzled too by the generously extended invitation to enter, however briefly, the dollar area—hopes for the future were perhaps even higher. There was promise in the air, if only because nobody knew how much might lie beyond the door that had just been opened.

The Schools Council produced its first declaration of policy in 1965, the year before Dartmouth. In it, English was earmarked as

one of three top priority areas and a research and development plan
of what now seems vast dimensions was sketched out. Its source of
inspiration was evident from its title—not *Project English*, but a somewhat' anglicized version, *The English Programme*. Schools Council
undertakings in general stressed "development", but in *The English
Programme* there was to be money also for "basic research". A Consultative Committee in Communication was set up to initiate and
co-ordinate research and this committee devised an ambitious series
of co-operative research projects that were to cover speech, reading,
writing, and comprehension throughout the years of schooling. From
that committee of under a dozen people, four members travelled to
Dartmouth. It must have been in their minds, and in the minds of
other delegates, that if *Project English* were to enter into a liaison
with *The English Programme*, there was no saying what progeny
might not be brought to birth.

Expectations of this kind from both sides of the Atlantic remained
unfulfilled. We can only speculate, of course, whether the reorienta-
tion of thinking about language and learning which is presented in
John Dixon's "growth model" could have been translated into the
kind of national reform envisaged by many Dartmouth planners, had
large-scale funding for educational innovation continued.

In retrospect we think not. Given the changes that had to occur
in the perception of teachers—about learning the subject, about
learners of the subject, about the teacher's interaction with learners—
we suspect that most members of the profession in both countries
needed time to think about the lessons of Dartmouth, the insights
of Dixon, and the new priorities only beginning, then, to emerge.
Continuation of large-scale funding in the United States could have
channelled post-Dartmouth thinking into unproductive moulds.

But continue it did not. The crisis in urban education in the
United States forced transfer of federal and foundation funds to
new priorities. Five years of teacher institutes and of *Project English*
research failed to convince a sufficiently large body of school and
public supporters that such enterprises were worth continuing when
choices had to be made. The "guns and butter" spending policies
of an American administration during the Viet Nam nightmare and
the associated economic and social chaos diverted attention to more
urgent national concerns. Education dropped from sight as a high

national priority; English education, except for specialized areas (bilingualism, for example), slipped low on the list within education.

In England the decline in a situation that had seemed so promising for research makes a more ordinary story. The funds newly made available proved inadequate to the demands made from all sides: the priority status accorded to English was gradually eroded in face of other urgencies. The Consultative Committee in Communication had drifted out of existence by the autumn of 1967, less than two years from its inception. Some of the projects it had fostered were carried to a conclusion but, as research projects will, they went their own ways with little co-ordination between them. The Schools Council policy in favour of practical outcomes, of direct use to teachers, was more firmly established: the Nuffield Foundation, by a partition agreement with the Schools Council, excluded work in English from its brief—and other foundations were, as ever, not in a position to offer a great deal of support.

We do not think the decline in large-scale projects today is altogether and necessarily a bad thing. If one looks for the impact of *Growth through English* in new and widespread curriculum designs, he looks in the wrong direction. We see rather the impact of the Dartmouth ideas—perhaps the Dartmouth ideal—in the enterprise of individuals: in the new insights of young teachers towards human communication that have been generated in North York, Canada; in the term-time work-shops held in a Calgary elementary school for teachers in a group of associated schools; in the network of teacher groups collecting and studying tapes of children's responses to stories that is part of the N.A.T.E./Schools Council *Children as Readers* programme; in the freedom to select a variety of teaching materials afforded teachers in the State of California; in the rapid movement of N.C.T.E. convention programmes from the large group lecture to interactive modes; in the scores of publications examining assumptions about growth in and through English, many of them written by teachers who neither participated in the conference nor were directly touched by it. Not all of these events can be traced to Dixon's book or to the conference that gave rise to it, but in the professional dialogue of recent years, both have stimulated much serious thinking. The climate in which educational change occurs has shifted dramatically since the book first appeared, but if national theorists have encountered troubled times, the "grass roots" dialogue continues vigorously in all three of our countries.

Changes in the social context of education

Our countries have seen widespread economic and social dislocation since *Growth through English* first appeared, and this unrest has had a significant impact on the thinking of teachers of English.

Critics of the Dartmouth Conference have rightfully criticized the deliberations for failing to relate the teaching of English to the socio-political contexts in which young people live today. Although partially redressed in the York Conference in 1971 and in a large variety of subsequent meetings on both sides of the Atlantic, we search our memories in vain for any high degree of sensitivity to the continuing crises that were shortly to follow the idyllic and isolated discussion in the White Mountains of New Hampshire: the desegregation controversies in American cities and the struggle for community control of education ("black teachers for black schools"), the crisis in values in the United States accelerated by growing rejection of the Viet Nam conflict and the revolt of students on campus and in schools; the American economic crisis which resulted not only in a growing surplus of qualified teachers but in staggering rates of unemployment among school and college leavers.

Of what value is a school certificate or a college degree if one does not emerge with a "saleable" skill? Such questioning initiated one major reversal of the traditionally cherished American assumption that schooling represented the surest way to scale the social and economic ladder. Leaders of American ethnic groups began to look on state-supported schools as a barrier rather than a bridge to social and economic mobility. The metaphor of the mosaic replaced that of the melting pot as new sensitivity to cultural pluralism emerged. ("Black is beautiful", an intent much more than a slogan, restored personal dignity to large numbers of Americans, and ethnic studies assumed new importance in American schools and colleges.) A group of powerful writers, somewhat patronizingly referred to as "the Romantic Critics" (Herbert Kohl, Jonathan Kozol, etc.) spoke out about the dehumanization of traditional schooling. Established American researchers questioned the impact of federal attempts at intervention in the educational process, indeed questioned the impact of the school on the lives of boys and girls (the Coleman Report, the Jencks Report, etc.). American taxpayers, expressing the traditional national concern with "efficiency", began to examine critically all expenditures for education, the movement fanned by a "more bang for the buck" psychology of many political leaders. "Back to basics" became a national trend, with mastery of reading and language of first concern. Out of such context in the United States came the stress on accountability— holding schools and teachers accountable for what pupils learn; introducing local, state, and national assessment of learning to check that pupils are progressing; using behavioural goals to guide curriculum content. If Canadian teachers seem to have been less affected by the extremes of these controversial issues, yet they were not immune.

On the other side of the Atlantic, in a context of housing shortage, continuing immigration, industrial unrest, rising prices, and the cost of entering the European Common Market, education has got into the news and stirred public opinion mainly on two issues: the thrust to establish a system of comprehensive secondary schools, and the attacks initiated by the *Black Papers* on what their authors conceived to be the evils of progressive methods of teaching.

The comprehensive policy, calling into question also the continued existence of the public schools, was, to delve deeper than the press coverage of these years, the outcome of a growing conviction that somehow social injustice was built into the educational system. More than twenty years have elapsed since the 1944 Education Act established the principle of "secondary education for all"; considerable optimism accompanied what was substantially the end of the eleven plus examination, and of the worst of the discriminations of the tripartite system. And yet, now in the seventies, things were clearly not working out right. Many of the clients themselves, the youngsters and their working class families, were coming to recognize that the idea of education as a ladder was a large-scale deception. No other image of it was offered with enough conviction and currency to make its point. Where immigrant children were concentrated, they suffered this same disadvantage and added others peculiar to themselves—language difficulties, cultural differences, racial prejudice.

The establishment of the Schools Council roughly coincided with a government decision to raise the statutory school-leaving age from 15 to 16 with effect from 1970. A campaign to prepare schools and teachers for this decree shared top priority with English (and Sixth Form Studies) in the Council's inaugural programme. It covered a wide range of fact-finding and attitude surveys, research and curriculum projects. One research was committed to discovering why and at what stage in their school careers some pupils become allergic to education. A large and costly curriculum project set out to investigate the desirability of teaching an integrated Humanities syllabus to 14 to 16 year olds, and went on to prepare and market teaching materials. Under Laurence Stenhouse's direction it developed as its method the raising of controversial issues for discussion by pupils under the neutral chairmanship of a teacher. It became itself a controversial issue, not least among teachers of English. There were other schemes for integrated studies of various kinds, the argument being that such courses were likely to be "more relevant to the needs and aspirations of pupils of average and below average ability" than the traditional courses that enshrined the subject disciplines.

In the debate that followed the word "relevance" became a banner word: from being an item in the sober inventory of evaluative categories used by G.C.E. examiners, it developed more interpretations, supportive or hostile, than any one word can usefully bear. The activity it mustered looks to us now like a desperate attempt to use curriculum change as one way of tackling the growing hostility of pupils in inner-city secondary schools to school and all that it stood for.

Where this hostility leads to crisis situations, English teachers are likely to be in the thick of it; the pressure is on them to break the impasse; they are where the problem is faced and that is where the solution is likely to arise. What the York 1971 Conference did, principally under pressure from its membership, was to recognize that teachers in this situation must not be left to fight their battles alone: those less directly confronting the problem must be brought to understand and respect the teacher's attempts at a solution. With tact as well as determination, subject associations like N.C.T.E. and N.A.T.E. can give active support.

In the field of Primary education, the main pursuit of the period has been "following up Plowden". Could the gospel of that Report be made to work in the toughest areas—those of poverty, poor housing, immigrant populations—if more money was spent there? A series of "action research" projects was set up to look for an answer. Many interesting measures were tried out, particularly with regard to the relationships between neighbourhood and school, parent and teacher, but if any final conclusion can be drawn from it all, it is one that corroborates the view emerging in the minds of many teachers facing the difficulties of the inner city secondary school; and a distinguished American commentator has made the same point concerning the American scene. Jerome Bruner, in an article he calls *"The Process of Education* Revisited",* writes: "A decade later, we realize that *The Process of Education* was the beginning of a revolution, and one cannot yet know how far it will go. Reform of curriculum is not enough. Reform of the school is probably not enough. The issue is one of man's capacity for creating a culture, society, and technology that not only feed him but keep him caring and belonging."

Perhaps education in our countries has differed most in the way schools are related to the context of parental and public opinion. In the United Kingdom, while schools have never been free for very long from outbreaks of press-inspired, sometimes ill informed, criticism (particularly, of course, in such matters as "why Johnny can't read"), the campaign mounted by the *Critical Quarterly* in the form of the *Black Papers in Education* was an unusual event. It served to unite many forms of antagonism to progressive ideas in education: indeed, the *Black Papers* as compilations were a hotchpotch that threw the serious in with the shoddy and exhibited none of the critical discrimination one might have expected from their editors. Beneath the many-faceted attack one genuinely held opinion came through powerfully and that was the élitist position summed up once and for all as "more means worse". The campaign may have exercised some influence upon the chain of events that led to the

---

* Jerome S. Bruner, *"The Process of Education* Revisited", *Phi Delta Kappan* (University of Harvard Journal), September 1971.

setting up of the government Committee of Enquiry into Reading and the Use of English in 1972—a chain of which the final link was the N.F.E.R. Report, *The Trend of Reading Standards.* Sir Alan Bullock, a historian—and therefore, perhaps, a version of Stenhouse's "neutral chairman"?—chaired the committee for its two-year's labours the outcome of which might be published any day now.

If the developmental view of learning advanced in *Growth through English* seems alien to some of the events we have described, it provides a continuing reminder that growth in language does not occur in isolation from the life experiences of boys and girls. The assault on traditional patterns of schooling has provided opportunity for individual teachers and schools to try out some of the Dartmouth ideas. Alternative patterns of education have begun to emerge: the open elementary school in America; the open classroom and the weakening of subject boundaries in the secondary school; the rise of alternative school structures; the widespread breakdown of the sequential four-year secondary programme in American schools into a plethora of short courses offered to pupils on an elective basis.

As we look back on the past decade, we see numerous signs that the dissatisfaction with traditional modes of instruction resulted from social and economic forces not envisaged at Dartmouth. But the existence of the "growth model" presented in John Dixon's book stimulated teachers to experiment with new approaches to language learning and literary education at a time when dissatisfaction with traditional models became widespread. Of all the changes, the shift in attitude towards subject matter seems likely to have the most long-range significance.

Changes in attitudes towards English

Clearly the post-Dartmouth dialogue among teachers of English has been marked by growing concern with student-centred education— with "learning" rather than with "teaching". The developmental view presented in *Growth through English* forced attention to the processes of interaction through which children acquire competence or expressiveness in language and strengthened conceptions of the teacher's obligation to guide and foster this development. Frank

Whitehead's dais has long since been disappearing from classrooms on both sides of the Atlantic.

The exercise of this growing concern has given us a clearer picture both of the particular role of language in learning and of the social constraints that may help or hinder its being used for that purpose. "Expressive language" as we would now want to describe it (whether in speech or writing) is at heart a function of the relationship of trust existing between the communicating parties. As teachers we know that such a relationship cannot be had on demand: it has to be cultivated in daily interaction. Its rewards are many; for expressive language is not only the medium in which we ask to be better known and understood and accepted (that is, in which we present the interpretation of the *I* that seeks a relationship of *we* with the listener), but it is also the medium in which we are readiest to take risks in the formulations we offer as to what the world is like and how its phenomena can be explained. Our version of the external world, the facts and theories we construct about it, must move on from the expressive stage, must be strengthened to enter debate, to profit from opposition, or merely to be communicated as useful to other people; but whenever a frontier is reached and our thinking becomes tentative, a return to expressive language with someone "in the context" and someone we trust is either necessary or likely to be very profitable.

The relationship of mutuality between teacher and taught has other implications. The home speech that children bring to school earns a new respect, is recognized for what it is worth as a continuing means of communication within a cultural group, and presents to the whole class a new opportunity for awareness and acceptance of speech differences. When speech differences become "interesting", a valuable new area is opened up to students' curiosity. Again, this relation of mutuality leaves the child the final arbiter of his own learning—in school, as he always has been out of school. The open classroom and individualized learning can do no more than mass instruction if teachers continue to deprive their students of that responsibility for their own learning.

"What kind of grammar should we teach?" is no longer a question that occupies the attention of many English teachers. And yesterday's concern with linguistic study has yielded to today's attention to the language development of pupils and to the uses to which language is put. If, as John Dixon asserts in his final essay in this book, Dartmouth directed too little attention to the processes of communication —to the uses of language in the participant's role as distinct from language in the role of spectator—it did unleash renewed concern with the pupils' own uses of language. Intense interest in self-discovery through language and in self-expression, with writing to realize oneself, has occupied the attention of teachers since that time.

Dynamic, interactive approaches to classroom experiences have become almost commonplace. Creative dramatics, almost unknown in America in the general English class beyond the primary-school level before the Anglo-American seminar, now is seen increasingly as a way to the exploration of values. Informal classroom talk, journal writing, creative experience with film, music, and graphic arts—all have become far more widespread.

Response to literary experiences of many kinds, not only the study of the best that is known and thought in the world, is again a major concern in planning a literary education and with it the opportunity to provide experiences with non-Western literary traditions, accelerated by a renewed awareness of the bicultural, bilingual heritage of the United States and the cultural plurality of England and Canada.

A notable change of attitude towards English in England in recent years has been the increasing interest in the place of English in the curriculum as a whole. Among practitioners, it is English teachers who have gone furthest in their exploration of the role of language in learning, and this has brought them to a point where they must consult with their colleagues in other subject areas. Progress towards the emergence within schools of a language policy across the curriculum may be slow, because subject barriers are often high to the point of rivalry, and time for consultation is barely provided for in time-tables and staff ratios. Certainly, to refer to John Dixon's last essay, we would hope that what he has to say about growth in language for participation would not be of interest to English teachers alone. To take up with him the argument as to priorities between spectator and participant uses of language would be merely to introduce questions of the territorial rights of curriculum subjects —a reversion to attitudes we are committed to leaving behind. It is

B

the total school experience of the student that matters, and with tact and patience we believe English teachers can use their knowledge and experience of language to promote the kind of consultation across subjects that will lead to a more unified learning experience for the student.

We believe that the ideas of Dartmouth in general and those expressed in *Growth through English* in particular have helped to shape these new attitudes towards English teaching. If external social, economic, and political events have forced teachers of English to interpret the "growth model" in a broader context than initially envisioned, so much for redressing a balance that should have occurred earlier. Increasingly, we feel, teachers recognize the crucial task of language in giving shape to all learning, whether in school or outside. The cross-Atlantic dialogue on the aims and methods of English teaching initiated at Dartmouth (1966) and continued at York (1971) and probably Banff (1975) has opened communication between teachers and researchers in all English-speaking countries and the fruits of this interchange are to be seen in cross-national studies, exchange visits to conferences and schools, the sharing of publications among several countries, and joint enterprises of the professional associations. May the dialogue continue unabated as long as it seeks better answers to the fundamental questions of concern to teachers everywhere.

Dartmouth opened with the question, "What is English?", which now seems to us a singularly unrewarding attempt to focus attention on the subject matter of the discipline. The conference responded with the answer, "English is whatever English teachers do". Today we think this response has clearly been extended to focus on our students themselves, and in this extension *Growth through English* has been a major influence. What is English? It proves impossible to mark out an area less than the sum total of the planned and unplanned experiences through language by means of which a child gains control of himself and of his relations with the surrounding world.

JAMES SQUIRE
JAMES BRITTON
1975

Chapter 1

A method of definition

With respect to the Master; that he be capable of and diligent in teaching to read, write and cast accounts. . . . With respect to the boys; that they can at least spell well.
(*Regulations for the English School,* 1704)

The tremendous pressure for a narrow and rigid standard of conformity in spelling, punctuation and usage that has sometimes squeezed nearly everything else out. . . .
(Al Kitzhaber, Dartmouth)

The English curriculum in the average secondary school today is an unhappy combination of old matter unrenewed and new matter that rarely rises above the level of passing concerns.
(*Freedom and Discipline in English,* 1965)

ENGLISH is a quicksilver among metals—mobile, living and elusive. Its conflicting emphases challenge us today to look for a new, coherent definition. Its complexity invites the partial and incomplete view, the dangerous simplification that restricts what goes on in the classroom. A map is needed on which the confusing claims and theories can be plotted.

In the map that emerges from the Dartmouth Seminar, one dimension is historical. Among the models or images of English that have been widely accepted in schools on both sides of the Atlantic, three were singled out. The first centred on *skills*: it fitted an era when *initial* literacy was the prime demand. The second stressed the *cultural heritage*, the need for a civilizing and socially unifying content. The third (and current) model focuses on *personal growth*: on the need to re-examine the learning processes and the meaning to the

1

individual of what he is doing in English lessons. Looking back over the history of our subject, we see the limitations in the earlier models and thus the need to reinterpret our conception of "skills" and "heritage".

The idea of a skill, a co-ordination of hand and eye in habitual, controlled action, seems at first sight perfectly suited to the rather narrow field of learning to read and write (to use language in the visual medium, not the oral). The word *skill* is still felt to have literal meaning here, rather than metaphoric. Yet on closer scrutiny it can apply literally only to minor elements of the total process, to the way our eyes scan the line perhaps, or the movements of our hands on the typewriter. The learning of correct spellings, of vocabulary, of punctuation habits, and the comprehending or use of longer and more complex sentences, are only "skills" in a vaguer, more extended sense; they are far from being exactly similar operations. If we have a persistent sense of their similarity, it arises from a muddled idea of their operation and a clear memory of the common teaching techniques mistakenly applied to some of them.

The first limitation of the skill model, then, is its tendency to assimilate the many different operations we learn in the course of beginning to read and write. Its major limitation, however, lies not in the area of English it chooses to sketch, but in the vast terrain it chooses to ignore. Nearly a century of emphasis on the skills of English has brought almost universal literacy in our countries—a literacy dissipated, for the most part, on the impoverished literature of the popular press (which grew in answer to it). We should not be surprised. Whenever the so-called skill elements of language learning are divorced from the rest of English, the means becomes the end. It has taken the Infant Schools, in their work with five- to seven-year-olds, to prove that a new and complex relationship is possible between the "skill" elements and the broader processes that prompt a child to use language in the first place. In the secondary schools we still invite defeat by putting the old "drills" alongside "imaginative" approaches to English.

The idea of English as a *cultural heritage* was clearly intended to fill the vacuum left by the skills model. Great literature offers, in Arnold's phrase, a criticism of life: what better could the children be reading? Here was a content for English that all could respect, a content moreover that linked the primary schools with the universities (from whom the proposal generally originated). "The Professor of Literature in a University should be—and sometimes is, as we gladly recognize—a missionary in a more real and active sense than any of his colleagues", said the 1919 Newbolt Report. Through literature all that was best in national thought and feeling could be handed on to a generation that knew largely slums and economic depression. In a happy way, too, the great writers would offer a variety of models on which the pupils' writing could be based.

One might point to the betrayal of this vision in a thousand class-rooms today where the "precious lifeblood of a master-spirit" becomes a series of inky marginal annotations and essay notes; but that would be to miss its real limitations. The central one concerns "culture". In the heritage model the stress was on culture as a *given*. There was a constant temptation to ignore culture as the pupil knows it, a network of attitudes to experience and personal evaluations that he develops in a living response to his family and neighbourhood. But this personal culture is what he brings to literature; in the light of it he reads the linguistic symbols (giving his own precious life-blood!). What is vital is the interplay between his personal world and the world of the writer: the teacher of English must acknowledge both sides of the experience, and know both of them intimately if he is to help bring the two into a fruitful relationship.

However, by re-emphasizing the text, the heritage model confirmed the average teacher in his attention to the written word (the point of strength in his training) as against the spoken word (the pupils' strength). It confirmed him too in presenting experience (in fictions) to his pupils, rather than drawing from them their experience (of reality and the self). But in doing so it set up tensions that have brought about its own collapse and a major reinterpretation of its noble aims.

To sum up what we learn from the historical dimension: looking at the first two models from the standpoint of child development, we can see they have exaggerated two areas at the expense of the rest and in so doing have distorted these areas themselves. It is as if the mapping had been done on an elastic sheet. During the skills era this was stretched till the operations specific to the written system of language became the centre of English. The heritage era put "skills" in their place as means to an end. But it failed to reinterpret the concept of "skills" and thus left an uneasy dualism in English teaching. Literature itself tended to be treated as a given, a ready-made structure that we imitate and a content that is handed over to us. And this attitude infected composition and all work in language. There was a fatal inattention to the processes involved in such every-day activities as talking and thinking things over, writing a diary or a letter home, even enjoying a TV play. Discussion was virtually ignored, as we know to our cost today on both sides of the Atlantic. In other words, the part of the map that relates a man's language to his experience was largely unexplored. (Think of the trivial essay topics that still result from this ignorance.) The purposes and pressures that language serves tended to be reduced to a simple formula—a lump sum view of inheritance.

A third model: language and personal growth

It is rather easy to be wise after the event; if we are to learn from our past mistakes we need to build English teaching on a second axis, based on our observation of language in operation from day to day.

When we do observe children as they learn to use language for their own purposes, surprising new areas of the map emerge that modify considerably our understanding of the earlier features. Take for instance the following entry in the diary of a ten-year-old boy:

1st April. Rainy with sunny periods. After breakfast I went out to get some newts. I got a large jar, washed it and put a stone in it, then went to poplar pond with a stone and a tin.

It was cold and very windy. After about an hour I had caught one femail newt. I was frozzen. I could hardly feel my hands they were so cold. I half filled the jar with water and a few water weeds and put the newt in. In the afternoon I tride to get another. I saw one just out of my reach. I waded out abit and foregot that I had a hole in one of my wellington boots. The water just flowd in. I didn't catch any more newts, and went home with a boot full of water. I'm going to try and get some more tomorrow and I hope I have better luck.

2nd. Very rainy dull and wet. To-day I made a fishing net, not to catch fish but newts. I caught six. I picked out the ones I thought best. I kept

three and let the others go. There were lots of newts in the pond t-day I
daresay they like this kind of weather.

The three newts I caught, two were a bright orange on the belly with
big black round spots all over, the other one was smaller and was a muddy
colour and its belly was a bright orange with very small spots on it. I
mean, the spots on this one were only on the belly not all over. The one I
got yesterday was a dark yellow ochre.

All afternoon I sat watching them, I think they are very interesting things.

It is difficult to remain indifferent to what the boy is saying: the
language invites a listener and speaks directly to him. (As he writes,
it is as if the boy has that sympathetic listener built imaginatively into
his mind.) In sharing the experience with the imaginary listener, he
brings it to life again, realizes it for himself. There are places where he
has worked to make something exact: "I mean the spots on this one
were only on the belly" ... " a dark yellow ochre." It is as if he is
listening and scanning what he has just said. At other places he has
wanted a different kind of communion with the listener—has stood in
a different relationship to his experience. "All afternoon I sat watching them, I think they are very interesting things." It is an open
invitation to join him in feeling that life is good. (Complex-sentence
hunters might agree that these two plain sentences are the sign not of
a failure in expression but of a rather fine type of control.) As an
English teacher one can see here a path that connects this writer's
intentions with Hemingway's stories of Nick. But earlier there was a
different growing point, when the boy chose to say, almost aside:
"There were lots of newts in the pond t-day I daresay they like this
kind of weather." There he was using language to draw observations
together and make a tentative hypothesis.

What, as English teachers, can we learn from such an extract?
This boy starts writing with a sense of having something worth
sharing. We can guess that he is used to having a sympathetic and
interested listener. He wants to make his experience real again, and
as he does so he makes discoveries. Using language in his case means
selecting some things for scrutiny and bringing things into order. So
the flux of experiences he encountered that day begin to take on a
meaning—a meaning which he treasures. We can be almost sure that
the language and the meaning are both *his*, not a product handed over
by the teacher. This is language in operation, not a dummy run, and

we have to make our classrooms places where pupils want to talk and write from impulses such as these.

This sample reminds us that language serves, and enables us to carry out, certain fundamentally human purposes. Even the private act of writing bears traces of the primary purpose in language, to share experience. The skills model is only indirectly aware of such a purpose: its ideal pupils might well be copy-typists. And that is ironical, since the insistence on correct spelling, etc., is avowedly in the interests of better communication, of unimpeded sharing! A heritage model, with its stress on adult literature, turns language into a one-way process: pupils are readers, receivers of the master's voice. How, we may ask, do these private activities of writing and reading relate to the stream of public interaction through language in which we are all involved every day, teachers as much as pupils? The heritage model offers no help in answering, because it neglects the most fundamental aim of language—to promote interaction between people. As a result drama, the literary form that directly embodies this interaction, has been interpreted as the study of texts, not acting them out. Current accounts of language as "communication" share the same weakness. They deal only in pre-formulated messages and ignore the discoveries we make in the process of talking and writing from experience, or in re-enacting an experience dramatically.

The fact is that in sharing experience with others man is using language to make that experience real to himself. The selection and shaping that language involves, the choices between alternative expressions so that the language shall fit the experience and bring it to life "as it really was"—these activities imply imaginative work. If we could observe all the occasions when a child uses language in this way, and put them together, we should have caught a glimpse of a representational world that the child has built up to fit reality as he knows it.

There is, then, a central paradox about language. It belongs to the public world, and an English classroom is a place where pupils meet to share experience of some importance, to talk about people and situations in the world as they know it, gathering experience into new wholes and enjoying the satisfaction and power that this gives. But in so doing each individual takes what he can from the shared store of experience and builds it into a world of his own.

When sceptical teachers ask, "Isn't that diary an example of the work of the rare few: aren't drills the only thing for the rest?" they must look again at our human purposes in using language. Recalling experience, getting it clear, giving it shape and making connections, speculating and building theories, celebrating (or exorcizing) particular moments of our lives—these are some of the broad purposes that language serves and enables. For days we may not work much beyond the level of gossip in fulfilling these purposes, but inevitably the time comes when we need to invest a good deal of ourselves and our energy in them. It is the English teacher's responsibility to prepare for and work towards such times. If instead of being *more* alert and sensitive to average pupils—more concerned with what they have to say, if only they can realize it—he neglects their day-to-day encounters with people and situations, then they will indeed be unlikely to turn to him when they are struggling to say something of importance.

It was for this reason that members of the Seminar moved from an attempt to define "*What* English is"—a question that throws the emphasis on nouns like *skills*, and *proficiencies*, set *books*, and the *heritage*—to a definition by process, a description of the activities we engage in through language.

How important these activities may be to us personally, how deeply they may affect our attitude to experience, is suggested by much of the best writing, drama and talk that goes on in English lessons. Here we see not only the intellectual organizing of experience that goes on in many other subjects, but also a parallel ordering of the feelings and attitudes with which pupils encounter life around them. For example, after an excited visit to a fine park, a class of eight-year-olds talked over their experiences. The wind in the trees, the lake, the swans, the boy who got mud up to his knees—these and many other things found their way into one or other of the pieces that the class wrote later. Janice wrote this short poem:

> The wind wiseled passed the trees.
> Pushing and puling the trees.
> The water triying to rech it.
> But still the trees remain.
> The wind stops but still the trees remain.

Pepol diey but still the trees grow biger and biger.
Flower diey but still the trees remain.

Here simple elements are drawn together into a vision of transience
and permanence: of things like the trees that persist, and of things
like man that wither; of the forces whose stress and strain we want
to withstand. Writing like this is an important moment of personal
growth.

The poem sharply reminds us of the power, always available in
language, to give meaning and order to the flux and fragments of
reality. Thus we make use of the system and order of language to
express the order we partly recognize in things. Until, like Janice, we
have written (or spoken), our recognitions and perceptions are less
articulate, less explicit. Once we have written, they become not
merely personal but shared, related to the socially made systems of
thought and feeling that our language expresses.

Of course, much of what pupils say and write and enact will be
less convincing in its insight than, say, Janice's work here. So will
much of our own work, for that matter. How can a teacher help
pupils engaged in so personal a task to weigh up what has been
achieved? All of us test the validity of what we have said by sensing
how far others that we trust have shared our response. An English
teacher tries to be a person to whom pupils turn with that sense of
trust. The sensitivity, honesty and tact of his response to what pupils
say will confirm their half-formed certainties and doubts in what they
have said. A blanket acceptance of "self-expression" is no help to
pupils and may well prove a worse hindrance to their growing self-
knowledge than a blunt and limited response from the teacher. The
more experienced the teacher is in these matters, the more he is able
to draw from the pupil the certainties (first) and later the doubts.

In every lesson where written work is read aloud to the class, or
where some pupils sit back while a group presents a piece of drama,
there is an opportunity for the teacher to draw from the audience
an appreciation of what was enjoyed, of what went home, and thus to
confirm in the individual writer or group a sense of shared enjoyment
and understanding. With a new class we begin by opening their eyes
to all they can achieve. And, as both the individuals and the class
become confident in their achievement, there will be moments when
with the teacher's help a sense of partial failure can be faced too.

For certainty about language is in a sense certainty about experience. Yet finding that others share our confidence in what we have said is only the foundation for work in language. As we mature we become increasingly aware that success in language is a partial business: as Eliot testifies:

... having had twenty years. ...
Trying to learn to use words, and every attempt
Is a wholly new start, and a different kind of failure
Because one has only learnt to get the better of words
For the thing one no longer has to say, or the way in which
One is no longer disposed to say it. And so each venture
Is a new beginning, a raid on the inarticulate. ...

(*East Coker*)

We can look on two levels at the source of our partial success. First, that of everyday experience: changes in oneself, changes in the surrounding world, and changes in one's relationship to others, all interpenetrate in the growing child or student to produce their own kind of serial curriculum. "World is crazier and more of it than we think, Incorrigibly plural." And at the level of language we can say this: we make for ourselves a representational world, sense out to the full its ability to stand for experience as we meet it, come up against its limitations, and then shoulder—if we dare—the task of making it afresh, extending, reshaping it, and bringing into new relationships all the old elements. Learning to use language continues so long as we are open to new experience and ready to adapt and modify the linguistic representation (the world) we have made for experience.

Knowledge and mastery of language

It is in the nature of language to impose system and order, to offer us sets of choices from which we must choose one way or another of building our inner world. Without that order we should never be able to start building, but there is always the danger of over-acceptance. How many teachers, even today, welcome and enjoy the power of young people to coin new words to set alongside the old order? How often do social pressures prevent us exercising our power to modify the meaning of words by improvising a new context, as in metaphor? Sometimes, it seems, our pupils are more aware than we are of the fact that language is living and changing; we could help them more often

to explore and test out its new possibilities. Inevitably, though, the weight of our experience lies in a mature awareness of the possibilities and limitations raised by the more permanent forms of order in language. There has already been an explicit case (at our own level) in this chapter. The question "What is English?" invites a different form of answer from, say, "What at our best are we doing in English classes?" If we wish to describe a process, *composition* for example, the first question will tend to suggest the finished product (the marks on the page even) rather than the activity of bringing together and composing the disorder of our experience. "What ... doing" will suggest nominal forms of verbs (bringing, composing) and thus help to keep activities in mind.

At a much simpler level members of the Seminar noted that some of us referred to "talk" in class, others to "speech". In order to see why, one might consider some of the contexts in which the words are used. "Talk" tends to be used of less formal occasions—"give a speech/give a talk". In some contexts "speech" implies accent or pronunciation—"good speech, classroom speech"; "classroom talk" may then be used as the generic term, even though in normal contexts we use "spoken and written, speech and writing" and not "talk". "Speech" seems to be rarely used today for verbal interaction, whereas we do say "we talked about it, talked it over, had a heart to heart talk". Tentatively, one might assume that those who preferred "talk" wanted to encourage informal interaction in class; those who preferred "speech" were perhaps hoping for sustained and organized utterance (rather than "chat"). Until differences like this are made explicit one may be trapped in a general uneasiness about what the other man means. Equally, in making the difference explicit we may begin to look more acutely at what goes on in class.

There is, then, a kind of knowledge or awareness about language that affects our power to think clearly and "to some purpose", in Susan Stebbing's words. Whatever the subject in the curriculum, the places where such knowledge can affect language in operation need to be more fully understood than they are at present. But the teacher of English will be particularly concerned with helping pupils, in the terms of one report, to "conceptualize their awareness of language". This seemingly cumbersome phrase was chosen with some care. "Conceptualizing", a verbal form, suggests *activity* on the part of the individual pupil, whereas "concepts" unfortunately can be thought of as *things*, reified objects to be handed over by the teacher. "Their awareness" points to a recognition already there in the pupil's thinking, not yet explicit or fully conscious perhaps, but something the alert teacher will notice and draw on.

The notion of gaining a new control over what we think by increasing our conceptual awareness of language in general has an obvious appeal to a gathering of intellectuals, not least when many of them are linguists! However, the final reports were cautious in their claims for such knowledge at the school stage. The first question at issue is when and how the knowledge becomes explicit. There was some agreement that the answer should apply to an individual rather than an age group. For if we teachers encourage a pupil to conceptualize, we should ideally be doing this at the point where the demands at the operational level of language have already given our pupil the sense that conceptualizing is needed. As experienced teachers we should see this demand emerging and be ready to help it on the way. In other words, our knowledge of the route ahead is not something to impose on the student—thus robbing him of the delight of discovery and maybe dissociating such discoveries as he does make from the systematic framework he "received" from us.

The second question was what knowledge if any *does* increase our mastery of language. As there seems to be little evidence, and some disagreement, one answer was to suggest further experimentation, with a determined effort to increase the teacher's awareness of the times when the demand for language concepts arises from the pupil but goes unrecognized at present. But the response of the majority of the Seminar was to reject the terms of the question and to ask instead for language knowledge that helps the pupil perceive himself, and for that matter Man, as in some sense the organizer of his experience. It was tentatively proposed that insights of this kind would come from a joint literary-linguistic discipline, the one investigating with more detachment the intuitions of the other. In terms of our map this was a healthy reminder that even over the next decade we may well see new territories being defined.

Dangers inherent in the third model

Whatever the current model for English, we shall have to recognize and face its weaknesses. Certainly the swing to process has its own dangers. The first is over-rejection. If the conventions and systems of written English do not come in the centre of the map, where do they come at all? The answer is obviously complicated, so there is a temptation to ignore the question. Let the pupils spell or not spell in the orthodox style, punctuate or not, struggle with ambiguities or not, make choices of structure or not . . . it is up to them! But though we can fight to modify conventions and systems, we cannot ignore them. Language remains a social instrument by which we share, fully or imperfectly, our preoccupations and interests. When deviance from the system becomes too great, interference may swamp and blot out the message. This very fact suggests a broad criterion to answer our complicated question. Where the pupil himself gives signs of being puzzled, disturbed or defeated by the forms of the written message which he is receiving or sending, the teacher should judge whether this is not the right moment to call his attention to the problem. We might note that the children's writing in this chapter includes several examples of deviance, but probably not enough to daunt readers experienced enough to take on this book. In class it might be a different matter: only experience can tell, for we put up with more interference when the message seems vital to us than when it is not.

The second danger, as U.S. members pointed out at the Seminar, is the tendency to over-simplification; of faith blundering from dull skills into the simple formula of "self-expression". Then the teacher can relax. Why trouble about people and things when the self is all-important? And, anyway, what criteria can—or dare—we use to assess what the self expresses? But this is to save the tree by cutting its roots. As people we exist and assert ourselves in response to our world (our family, neighbourhood, teachers . . .). The sense of our own reality is bound up with our sense of theirs, and both intimately depend on an awareness built up through language. For, of all the representational systems, language is the best fitted to make a running commentary on experience, to "look at life with all the vulnerability, honesty and penetration [we] can command". In an English classroom as we envisage it, pupils and teacher combine to keep alert to all that is challenging, new, uncertain and even painful in experience. Refusing to accept the comfortable stereotypes, stock responses and perfunctory arguments that deaden our sensitivity to people and situations, they work together to keep language alive and in so doing to enrich and diversify personal growth.

To sum up: language is learnt in operation, not by dummy runs. In English, pupils meet to share their encounters with life, and to do this effectively they move freely between dialogue and monologue— between talk, drama and writing; and literature, by bringing new voices into the classroom, adds to the store of shared experience. Each pupil takes from the store what he can and what he needs. In so doing he learns to use language to build his own representational world and works to make this fit reality as he experiences it. Problems with the written medium for language raise the need for a different kind of learning. But writing implies a message: the means must be associated with the end, as part of the same lesson. A pupil turns to the teacher he trusts for confirmation of his own doubts and certainties in the validity of what he has said and written; he will also turn to the class, of course, but an adult's experience counts for something. In ordering and composing situations that in some way symbolize life as we know it, we bring order and composure to our inner selves. When a pupil is steeped in language in operation we expect, as he matures, a conceptualizing of his earlier awareness of language, and with this perhaps new insight into himself (as creator of his own world).

Chapter 2

Processes in
language learning

In general, it is a mistake to assume that—past the very earliest stages—much of what the child acquires is acquired by imitation. This [assumption] could not be true on the level of sentence formation, since . . . most of what he produces . . . is new.

(Chomsky: *Formal Discussion*)

. . . the social structure generates distinct linguistic forms or codes and these codes essentially transmit the culture and so constrain behaviour . . . there will arise distinct linguistic forms, fashions of speaking, which induce in their speakers different ways of relating to objects and persons.

(Bernstein 1965)

In a sense a child over-abstracts at first as well as under-abstracts: he cuts his world into a few simple categories that cover too much and discriminate too little. . . .

(Moffett, Dartmouth)

Dialogue inside grows out of dialogue with others. This is how society penetrates our thinking.

(H. Rosen, Dartmouth)

BECAUSE our concern is language in operation, we need to understand the processes involved in language learning. Unfortunately, from the standpoint of theory these are still areas of ignorance rather than knowledge. We can do little more than sketch the regions where investigation is going on and where more should be encouraged. Members of the Seminar from both sides of the Atlantic agreed that there had been a failure to set up adequate research institutes for such investigations. In the first place these needed to be grounded

14

firmly in the classroom, with teachers actively involved. But though the roots should be the schools, what arises needs help from psycho-linguists, socio-linguists and child psychologists, for example. An institution—a centre—is needed where teams of this kind can collect and with which teachers can keep in touch. A working relationship between the schools and the centre would help to produce working knowledge and awareness. (For "knowledge", we note, has suffered unduly from its reification.) A major function of research at such a centre would be to confirm or modify the teacher's preconceptions, to point our attention to new kinds of awareness, and to help us (when we feel the need) to make some awareness more explicit. But we teachers must ask the questions too.

The repertoire of structures

Thus, as we observe the language that children use, both in speech and writing, we may wonder how much of the basic structure they have learnt. For some time the linguists have maintained that the normal child of five or six is "a linguistic adult". "He controls, with marginal exceptions if any, the phonemic system of his language; he handles effortlessly the grammatical core; he knows and uses the basic contentive vocabulary" (Hockett). Observations and analyses of children's speech and writing by Strickland, Loban and Hunt clearly support this claim and suggest that the limited structures often encountered through casual observation are probably only a small part of a latent repertoire. The achievement of this repertoire is a remarkable example of self-education which the schools do well to build on. "What the child has learned already he has learned under the pressure of the necessities and pleasures of daily living. If school is to continue the processes already started it must stir the same kind of pressure and kindle the same excitements." It seems essential to know how a child achieves this mastery; as yet, however, the best that scholars can do is to point to the likely factors affecting language development. These include "the amount, variety, and quality of language heard and used in the family (in conversation, table talk, stories, etc.); the variety of experience including much non-threatening, self-enhancing interaction with other people and opportunity to verbalize this experience; encouragement and oppor-tunity for self expression, not only in language but in other ways"

c

(Loban). There is a remarkable agreement between these factors and some ideas on school independently suggested to the Seminar by David Holbrook (p. 95).

Perhaps this is the place to mention the danger, on the other hand, of restricted linguistic judgements. For instance, the repertoire of structures used in speech shows an increasing complexity as children grow older and develop more control of language. On the face of it, then, one might use growing complexity of repertoire as evidence to support a particular programme of instruction in language (given the appropriate controls). But this is to forget that complexity may be well used or badly used to organize experience. Members of the Seminar were sharply critical of claims, based on such evidence, for *sentence-stretching* by adding modifiers or by sentence synthesis.

Language switches

Nevertheless, the effect of modern linguistic research is to reinforce our awareness of the complexity of resources demanded by modern societies. Infant speech is perhaps best thought of as "an undifferentiated matrix out of which will emerge many highly specialized language functions" (Whitehead). A major hurdle for young children with a strong local or social dialect is learning to accommodate to the standard English in which all their books are written. And we now begin to see this as only one of a whole set of language switches that a pupil must gradually learn to make as he copes with new situations and takes on new social roles. The language of home, he learns, differs in significant ways from the language of the classroom; the language of the classroom differs from that of a school assembly; stories differ from talk; textbooks about a new subject may appear to have invented a new language. It can all be very puzzling. The failure of schools to help pupils gradually to assimilate the complicated varieties of English in modern use explains why in secondary schools today so much of language "looks at pupils across a chasm".

Thus in learning to read, children are in danger of feeling a sudden discontinuity, a change from the familiar dialect forms to forms which may (at worst) have been rarely heard or which feel alien. A linguistic barrier can be set up in this manner and in the majority of cases it need not be. At least four stages should be observed:

(a) much enjoyable listening to standard English—assimilating it with satisfaction through stories told by the teacher and later through her reading stories too;

(b) reading aloud by teacher and child of the child's own stories, told in his own language and preserved in that form by the teacher who wrote them down;

(c) reading stories in standard with accompanying talk;

(d) reading standard on his own.

The length of each stage will be related to the differences between dialect and standard forms. But in any case "learning to read and write leaves the child alone with language in a way which differs from his previous experience. This should not be made a sudden transition. The new activities should be preceded, accompanied and followed by talk."

So much for learning to assimilate the standard forms written by somebody else; but what of speaking and writing for oneself? Of the two, writing is the simpler issue, because there is, broadly speaking, only one British form (the one used in this book) and American standard English differs hardly at all. There are hopes (in need of experimental testing) that under the influence of much reading, the written forms used by a pupil will change to standard. This demands teachers who realize that "the concept of original sin, linguistically speaking, is untenable" (Marckwardt)—that dialect is personal and valuable, not an incorrect version of standard. The alternative method of writing drills seems difficult to motivate, of dubious effectiveness, and possibly of damaging effect. Pupils need to associate standard English, whether heard or read, with pleasure rather than with drudgery or uncertainty. And in the interim, while the accommodation is being made, the teacher makes a decision on the priority to be given to the human purposes in language. A West Indian, about thirteen years old, comes to your school, for example. Does her experience come first or the "correctness" of her English? Suppose she writes this in answer to your assignment:

In ten years times I'll remember a picture of my dad who I haven't seen for 5 years. My dad when to America in 1958, when there and haven't been back. I when to see him there from since then I haven't seen him.

He took a picture of the family and leave it when he were going, from

since then I have that picture and alway will to remember the last time I
saw him and to remember those day when he were near.

That picture is home in a frame and every night before I go to bed I take
up the picture and look at it sometimes a strong feeling come over me and
just start to cry it make me think if the family will ever by like the old
photograph which in that frame on the wall.

For some years I ask my mom why don't dad come and see us no more,
she just says some day why some day I ask. In replied she just answer you
have to find out for yourself. I said to her mom are you afraid of something
are you holding something from me. replied no. So one day I ask my nany
is mummy and daddy had a quarrel why he dont come to see me no more ?. . . .

Whatever our attitude to the forms of language, spoken or written,
we have to leave the way open for things of importance to be said—
to retain the position of trust. And that means ignoring correctness
and dialect forms at such moments, because for the pupil the
experience is all-important.

Why is the problem so complex? Because, though it lies in the
linguistic domain, dialect is fundamentally a social matter. Language
of course asserts our membership of a speech fellowship. To members of lower status groups, then, standard is a prestige dialect spoken
by upper status groups or classes. The reverse of this view is that
dialects of lower status groups are "sub-standard". In a paper too
important to be briefly summarized here, Labov* has pointed to a
major difference of attitude between status groups in New York.
Lower class speakers showed little or no consciousness of external
standards of correctness in spoken English: as one said, "How can I
speak any other way than I do?" Lower middle class speakers have
the highest group recognition of such external standards "as an
inevitable accompaniment of [their] upward social aspirations and
upward social mobility".

Notions of "correctness" and sensitivity to "correct" speech forms
have a class bias, therefore. Often they will produce a counter-
pressure in the school or neighbourhood, so that "the adolescent
peer group exerts strong pressure against any deviation in the
direction of middle class norms."

So, in a world of insecurity and status preoccupations, "one uses
the language which helps to preserve one's life, which helps to make

* *Social Dialects and Language Learning*, N.C.T.E., Champaign, Illinois, 1964.

one feel at peace with the world, and which screens out the greatest amount of chaos", as Ralph Ellison said (*Social Dialects and Language Learning*). But "if you can show me", he goes on, "how I can cling to that which is real in me, while teaching me the way into the larger society, then I will . . . drop my defences and my hostility . . ."

Let us be clear that it is a case of teachers liberating themselves as well as their pupils, and that to do so they need to draw on linguistics, psychology and sociology for a conceptual framework that will explain the processes involved. Thus:

(a) A dialect often, maybe generally, carries indications of social or class status.

(b) When we speak it we identify ourselves with the group who use it, whether Tynesiders or Harlem Negroes.

(c) Standard spoken forms are inevitably less well defined than standard English proper (the written form); the question of acceptability is more open since there is no institution (like the publisher) concerned with producing an acceptable standard, and no simple method like consulting the dictionary, for example.

(d) Both local or social dialect and standard spoken English will vary in phonology, syntax, morphology, and lexis according to whether the situation in which they are used is formal or informal. In his New York study of certain status markers in pronunciation, Labov has shown that a workman may use the prestige form quite frequently in formal situations, and that middle class speakers frequently use unconsciously in casual speech the very form that they explicitly stigmatize. So there may be overlapping stratification of local dialect and standard, or there may not: the evidence so far is fragmentary.

(e) Whatever the dialect, learning to use a regional variety of standard spoken (which even in Britain is acceptable in discourse on educational, governmental topics, etc.) involves wanting to be accepted by speakers already using it. Social segregation in more or less extreme forms exists in both countries and while it does, the children and young people who suffer from it are unlikely to see adequate reasons for changing their dialect. For example, "unless the white community shows an active will to accept and integrate the Negro citizens, they cannot possibly have a full-scale motivation for learning standard English. The school can give them only a surrogate for the teaching they should be getting from their white friends and neighbours. Those who learn standard English may still be snubbed and rejected for their colour. They have put in a great deal of effort to lose their Negro identity yet they have still failed to acquire a white identity" (Haugen, *Social Dialects*). Social change must precede educational change in this case.

(*f*) Where people of different social background mix fairly freely, the need to use mutually acceptable forms produces accommodations—and thus produces teachers who sometimes informally use local forms, and pupils who on more formal occasions use a variety of standard. (One can see this at work with B.B.C. television interviewers.) The sympathy, respect and emulation stirred by the school and what it stands for in such a community will provide the necessary preconditions for pupils learning to use standard forms alongside their own dialect. If the streaming or grouping system in the school accentuates social differences, on the other hand, accommodation is much less likely.

(*g*) Most pupils who speak a dialect do learn to assimilate varieties of standard that they hear and read. In a sense, then, they have already mastered the standard forms as well as their own: all they have to do is to move on from passive mastery of standard to active use of it. This suggests that the change is not impossible. But equally, "all scholars are agreed that it is harder to keep two similar languages apart than two very different ones" (Haugen). Teachers with an adequate awareness of the problems of switching back and forth will be less concerned to penalize "mistakes" (inefficient learning after the event) and better prepared to see that the pupil is *incidentally* reminded of the standard form in the course of school work. We need more evidence on the process, the stages, and the timing involved.

(*h*) However willing they are, some pupils may find it difficult to pick up standard forms of spoken and written. What to do next is not clear. Can drama help? Should second language drills be used—and if so, with what motivation? Experiments will help to clarify our answers here.*

Restricted roles for language

Teachers and linguists alike have been accustomed to think of dialect in over-simple terms. Labov points out that "linguistics has made the most progress in analysing the cognitive component; but many elements in language . . . are imbued with non-cognitive values as well". Thus the dialects of the urban working classes choose certain levels and elements from experience and imply evaluations of them. Standard and social dialects are not different ways of saying the same thing—are not a set of equivalent "codes". Each style of life, implying as it does certain kinds of relationship between people and certain attitudes to experience, results in the habit of selecting in certain ways from the cognitive and non-cognitive possibilities of a language. Thus Basil Bernstein has drawn our attention to the manner of speech among some working class boys in London—how predictable their utterances are, how much relies on implicit meaning and extra-verbal signals. As one index of what is going on, he looks at the boys' use of "they": the word has a characteristic vagueness. It does not necessarily refer back to particular people, or even to groups like "the bosses". The lack of an antecedent implies that "we" all know what is referred to, so it would be redundant to elaborate. In a sense, therefore, "they" is being used to reinforce "the community of interests generated by WE". There are some similarities with the (under) conceptualizing of young children—the way for example a toddler may use "a mummy" to refer to almost any person other than a young child. The concept looks to us highly abstract but is felt by the child to be very concrete. Gradually he will learn to refine on this concept—to distinguish among girls, young ladies, married women, mothers, motherly people, etc. But as Bernstein comments, this development of a series of levels of abstractions seems to be missing in the use of "they" that he reports. This is only one of many features in what he calls a "restricted code".

Of course everyone uses language in this way at times, in talk with intimate friends perhaps. But pupils limited in their language

---

* Nelson Francis (see page 115) is at present engaged in such an experiment, using various methods to help college students gain a mastery of standard forms.

ST. MARY'S COLLEGE OF EDUCATION
FALLS ROAD, BELFAST, 12.

strategy to such a restricted code are poorly equipped to make meaning explicit to themselves or others. Consequently they enter school with an enormous disadvantage and are unlikely to recover from it—unless we can devise teaching methods that take their special needs into account.

But the process is more than linguistic in its roots and its consequences. The linguistic limitation "originally elicits and later reinforces a preference in the child for a special type of social relation . . . limited in terms of verbal explicitness. . . ." The social "dialect" restricts the roles a child can take on, and restricts his image of himself. "A change of code involves changes in the means whereby social dentity is created." As Bernstein said in the NATE Bulletin (11·2), 'We [teachers] are asking a lot of these children."

"If there is an imaginative, creative, adventurous potential within our children, then there is a new responsibility for teachers of English (far more than for other teachers in the school system) which isn't a simply pedagogic responsibility, because the school in fluid societies is an agent of cultural change. New identities are being created as children become involved in the school system, and a symptom of this change in identity will in fact be presented to the teacher in terms of that child's difficulties and tensions, initially in English." We might relate this general comment from research to a statement by a seventeen-year-old Yorkshire schoolboy in *The Excitement of Writing*.* (American readers should note that in the U.K. only a rather academic minority of pupils normally stay on into the "Sixth Form" after reaching the age of sixteen.)

'The problem of speech facing a sixth former in a working class area is only a relatively minor one. It is a reflection of the much greater complexities he faces in having to live two lives . . ."

At present this is a new field. We can do little more than outline the scope for teachers and researchers to look into the varieties of English that pupils start school with, meet there, and need to develop. One can think of such research as looking in three directions (not mutually exclusive).

—First, at variations in the way children's language impedes and enlarges the relations in which they can stand with respect to

* The Excitement of Writing. ed. A. B. Clegg (Chatto & Windus) 1964.

experience, and in particular the cognitive and affective quality of those relations. Here Bernstein's present work is central, though it also includes other directions.

—Second, at the way language needs to vary as the form of experience changes (in the nature of the elements isolated and the structure and type of their relations to each other). Work recently set up in England and Wales under the Schools Council is directly related to this: at present it is designed to cover speech among pupils eleven to eighteen, and writing from eleven to eighteen in the different school subjects and for general purposes.

—Third (and intimately associated with both the others) at the way pupils' language varies with their social relationship to the listener(s) or potential reader. Here the Seminar agreed on the urgent need for further research into the dynamics of groups in class, with investigation of questions such as the following:

(a) How does children's language change in changing group situations, e.g. problem-solving as against gossiping?

(b) What differences does the presence of the teacher make?

(c) How far does size of group affect the style of utterance?

(d) What kinds of language emerge from the carrying out of a common task, self-initiated as against teacher-initiated?

The vital need is "to use the evidence of speech variation (and varieties of writing) ... to infer the deeper, underlying processes which must be understood if we are to solve the urgent problems of the urban schools" (Labov). For children come to school limited in the social roles they can play and the situations they can cope with. As far as language is concerned, we can see the school as a special opportunity to meet a wide variety of situations and to take on (in play and in earnest) a variety of roles within them. As they do so, the children learn (under the teacher's guidance) to draw on those levels and develop those features of language that will help them to entertain and control the experience.

Language enabling new roles to be developed

Take, for example, the way children use language in carrying out certain tasks—a subject to which the psycho-linguistic research of Luria and Vygotsky has brought new awareness. Where the manipulations required are complex (requiring step by step procedure) and planning is called for, it seems that language has an important function: young children who can talk over the steps and operations as they carry them out have a better chance of succeeding, even when their companion says nothing. Here is Stephen, just under three but from a linguistically rich home, learning to use language in this way while playing with his trains. (His mother's responses are in italics.)

That's going on . . . on . . . on the carriages. That's going to go next to the carriages—you see?
And we shall put on the brake you see?
We shall put on the brake.
We got the diesel trains haven't we?
I play with that, then Jonathan played with that train and then I played with those two trains. And he played with Punch and Judy when Daddy was ready to go to work.
Did he? Yes, he did. . . .
. . . Then fall down like this . . .
Oh that's going to go—on this do you see?
And then it's got a [*inaudible*] like that.
Mine's a block engine isn't it?
And that engine is going to be on that train you see.
And if you do have a truck in there it won't work.
Won't it? No. *Why not?* Cos it won't.
There's two engines. There's lots of trains.

I want my socks off—the fire will warm them won't it?
Yes. My nose was a bit runny so wiped it on that.
Did you? That will warm it up—there—I've put them my socks on the fireguard so the fire will warm them up you see. *Oh—*
Look! you see? The book shouldn't be under there should it?
No! No! [etc.].

Stephen's language is already beginning to move flexibly from one purpose to another. It precedes and accompanies his activities; it recalls past events, putting them in a simple sequence; it helps in the rejection of certain behaviour ("if you do" . . .)—though an explicit cause and effect relation is evaded. His mother's presence seems unimportant, until we think of the "you sees". Her remarks are highly redundant; when her language *is* used for cognitive purposes, it fails to elicit the appropriate response.

In the silent classrooms of the old infant schools, children who had not already developed these purposes and procedures in their play at home were probably retarded in the performance of all but the simplest school tasks. One answer was to drill, to simplify the task through handing the planning over to the teacher. There is something symbolic in the method: "don't teach children to plan, plan for them". The alternative is to provide at school similar situations to the one Stephen enjoyed. Play has long been recognized as an essential part of work in the best primary schools; what we need now is an increased awareness of the language purposes it encourages and develops. As part of his current research, for example, Bernstein has developed, with the help of the teachers, experimental games and play directed to helping young children break out of restricted codes. This is a field where a survey of fruitful ideas already in operation would help many infants' teachers working with children from linguistically impoverished homes. So would a reduction in the size of classes, which at 35–40 often make impossible the individual attention that Stephen was getting.

We must recall that the role of English here is fundamental to social life. Planning procedures, built on the sort of work Stephen was doing, enter into a great deal of adult behaviour, often at points where we are no longer aware of them, because their operation is not conscious—as in starting and driving off in a car. And this is a simple example: for one that is more complex, consider the child who does not "know how to start his story". What operations has he to develop to get under way? Will sitting silent be a help—or would talking it over with the teacher, or a classmate, or a group of children? What sort of nudging goes on when a good teacher helps the child to make a start?

Perhaps the switch from talking over an operation with someone to talking it over with yourself (thinking it over) is part of a general switch that many young children learn to make, more or less for themselves. Stephen's "you see" ("won't it, isn't it, haven't we") represents a half-way stage. The address to another person is becoming redundant and so are her replies. This marks an enormous gain in linguistic independence. For in conversation (the elementary form of language) a child's responses are to some extent structured (in behaviour and linguistic form) by the need to respond to what his experienced companion has just said. Conversation permits a

rapid and continuous feedback of signs that show how effective
language has been—signs in words and signs in movement (facial
gesture particularly). Deprived of the sight of the other person's face,
as in telephoning, children may find talk difficult until they learn to
use the linguistic clues to response (even something as simple as
"yes ... yes ... yes ..."). The feedback helps us all to modify,
repeat, replan or continue what we were saying. We see this at work
in class discussion and, at a higher level, in Socratic dialogue. But
monologue throws us back entirely on our own linguistic strategies—
and this is a matter of something more than vocabulary and sentence
structure (though both are included). In some way we need to internalize the other speaker in the dialogue. The child learns to take on
more than one role: asking questions and answering them, one might
say, or giving himself good advice. (Stephen illustrates this process.)
Telling a story, writing, and giving a talk are just a few of the forms
of monologue we may need to master and each will demand a set of
special if overlapping strategies. And we are only at the beginning of
realizing the significance to human understanding of being able to
internalize the language and viewpoint of the other speaker. (Think
at the university level of the simulation of international conflicts or
conferences, with students taking the roles of prime ministers,
generals, etc.)

One day a girl of six on her way to school saw a kitten killed by a
lorry. Such an experience is hard to take, whatever way we look at it.
The girl worked for a long time that day, drawing and (with her
teacher's help) writing beneath each of the drawings. Strung together,
this is what she wrote.

The sun is waving goodbye to you all.
The moon is coming out said the kitten to himself.
Today I hear the thrushes sing on my lawn said the kitten to himself.
The thrushes are in the garden and the kitten is in the garden.
The kitten is coming to church said the children.
The kitten is coming home said the children.
Goodbye said the children.
The kitten is coming to bed said the mice.
The kitten is coming to town said all the kittens.
The lorry is coming to squash the kitten said the mice.
The lorry is coming to squash the kitten said the children.

The kitten is squashed.
And that is the end of my story about the kitten.

Often the heart of a child goes out to a kitten, seeing there an image of itself. But children learn to be many people, many creatures. Has this girl perhaps learnt in the end to face and suffer the kitten's mutilated death and yet to see that experience in all its variety stretches away beyond?—that life goes on; one lives in other roles.

We come here to the border country between scholarship and the intuitive understandings of observant and sympathetic teachers. Ideally the one kind of evidence should feed the other. Teachers who can help their pupils to develop through language may draw attention to unsuspected potentialities. We might recall Joan in David Holbrook's *English for the Rejected*: timid, plain, with thick pebble glasses. Her I.Q. was 76; there was nothing surprising perhaps in her primary school record—"has no originality or imagination". Yet after a year's encouragement to creative work in language and drama, she wrote this (in the course of the exam):

> *A poem.*
>
> A little yellow bird sat on my window sill
> He hop and poped about
> He whiseld he cherped.
> I trid to chach my little yellow brid
> but he flew into the golden yellow sun,
> O how I wish that was my yellow brid.

Work such as this has given us a new right to talk about the creative potentialities of *all* children. Consider not only the beauty but the complexity of Joan's achievement. The bird is alive, quick and jaunty; we feel her longing too. But despite its immediacy the poem surely suggests another level for the yellow bird and the golden yellow sun—a level not to be spelt out, but just as certainly to be felt. For language, like drama, has the capacity to bring elements from experience into a structure that stands for life not merely in particular but in general. Indeed it is clear that in the earliest river valley civilizations men learnt to handle generality not in explicit, rational terms, but through myth—creative stories, poems and dramas. So (perhaps?) as they develop, all pupils need to explore their power—through language and dramatic movement—to bring a new, simplifying order to the complexity of life. This might be called the poetic work of language (but an undifferentiated poetry rather than the specialized genres of contemporary society).

What we see here is one pole of a continuum. At this end, deeper levels of the self are realized and composed; at the other, language takes us out to encounter and bring to explicit order the external world. Neither is simple.

> We had the experience but missed the meaning,
> And approach to the meaning restores the experience
> In a different form ...
>
> (*The Dry Salvages*)

Pupils, like adults, need to talk over new experiences, returning to them again and again maybe, finding new elements and connections. The potential meaning of an experience—an outing, a visitor, an experiment—is not always clear at once. It needs to be worked over, "realized" again through language, shared and modified perhaps in the way we apprehend it. And new experiences are sometimes old ones seen in a new light ("Tintern Abbey"). So the toughest, least articulate teenager may be putting up a shield to keep experience at bay (as he thinks) and preserve his balance against its threatening effects. Talking it over, thinking it over, and (as confidence is gained) writing, can be natural parts of taking account of new experience (cognitively and affectively).

The processes described as "resolving inner tensions", "taking account of experience", "coming to terms with it", and so on, share some characteristics with the work of an artist. Like the artist, children engaged in these activities are adopting a special role to their selves and to their experience, the role in some sense of spectator rather than participant. How everyday and yet fundamental this role may be is suggested by an illustration from James Britton:

"I think we can distinguish two ways in which a wife may recount to her husband when he comes home what the children have been doing. The one is quite ordinary and frequent. She goes over the events because she knows he is interested: and though what he hears may inspire him to vague dispositions to act or to decide, they are so vague and so remote that they do not switch him from the role of spectator to that of participant. If hairbreadth escapes are part of the story, once he has been assured that the children are safely tucked up in bed and none the worse, he will even savour the excitement of fright about these events—an experience quite different from the fears of participant. And the wife who tells him the tale savours it now in a way she certainly did not, as a mother, earlier in the day when they were actually happening.

And there are other, rarer occasions when the wife, after tactfully (and perhaps tactically) talking about other things, begins to tell a different kind of story about the events of the children's day. She tells it in a different way because she is herself still a participant, wanting to influence her husband to act this way rather than that. And he listens as a participant because he is called upon to act and to decide: he has not now the specta-tor's freedom to enter fully into the events of the story and savour the emotions: instead, it is *his own* role he must play, mastering his feelings if need be, and summoning his judgement." *(The Arts in Education)*

The role of spectator—of an attentive, immersed onlooker—is thus a link between the child and the artist. Again we become aware of the work children have to do (through language) before they can draw on the mature writer. If their talk and writing in the role of spectator does not reach occasionally beyond the level of gossip, how can they be expected to reach up beyond that level into what the play or the novel is saying. Yet it is at the level of gossip that we all start, and with many children the classroom offers them their only chance to move towards a fuller sense of what talk and reflection can offer. For "detached evaluative responses, though less intense, tend to be more widely comprehensive than the evaluation that precedes participation. One views the event in a more distant perspective and relates it to a more extensive system of information, beliefs and values. And this detached evaluative response undoubtedly possesses the utmost importance in building up, confirming and modifying all but the very simplest of our values. . . . If we could obliterate the effects on a man of all the occasions when he was 'merely a spectator' it would be profoundly to alter his character and outlook"* (Denys Harding). When life is felt as immediate and particular, our work in this role is closest to the artist; as it moves towards generality it moves closer to the thinker. Perhaps English holds the middle ground. Certainly there are times when the two are not felt to differ. Consider this passage by a sixteen-year-old girl about her mother:

* "The Role of the Onlooker," SCRUTINY, 1937.

". . . It is sad that I should only recently realize that sympathy she has in her, how easily I can talk to her of my feelings, and how sympathetic and understanding she is, and how willing she would be to help me out of my difficulties even though it may be against her own principles. It makes me feel ashamed that I should have less affection for her than I did as a young child. Perhaps it is the loss of my complete dependence on her and the awareness of my mental independence or the maturity of my emotion and that what I took for deep love and utter devotion in my early childhood was nothing but a superficial emotion. A young child has to love someone and I had no-one else on whom to place my affections. Or maybe we have only a certain capacity for affection and though at one time we may lavish it all on one person as soon as others come along we take from the first person to give a little to the others. I do not know the answer, only that all emotions and qualities change, develop or mature and that time leaves nothing untouched. . . . I am afraid not only of losing my physical youth but any childishness I still have. . . ."

Pupils with their own experience of the role of spectator have the power, then, to draw from the artist and thinker new insights into life. When it speaks to them like their own work, the mature writer's poem or story or philosophizing helps to give new order and meaning to parts of their own experience. But as the writer realizes experience more fully, keeping the language in touch with far more of live feeling and human interaction, children who become involved in his "work" (as we rightly call it), giving their share of creative work in re-enacting its processes for themselves, may gain a new richness in facing experience.

To sum up: an understanding of the processes involved in developing a mastery of language becomes vital when it sharpens the teacher's awareness of a pupil's potentialities, problems and limitations. In the pre-school years, almost all children miraculously acquire the basic resources in phonology and structure of the local or standard dialect. But some children also acquire through parents and neighbourhood a restricted strategy for the use of these resources, for behind language lies the force of social relationships and where these are critically limiting, language is too. Nevertheless, one starts in teaching from a respect for each pupil as he is, and that means for what expresses his identity, notably his language. "One of the most intimate possessions of a person is his dialect. . . . The identification of the child with his community and his relationship to it must be protected" (Wilt). The principal aim is to build on the method of language learning by which he has already accomplished so much. The classroom is a place for taking on new roles, facing new situations —coming to terms in different ways with new elements of oneself and new levels of human experience. In the course of doing so, with the teacher's encouragement and guidance, language is *incidentally* adapted to the new role, especially when the teacher can avoid serious discontinuity. Thus the movements from spoken to written, from dialect to standard, from kinds of dialogue to kinds of monologue, are all potentially points of rupture—of breakdown in confidence, in acceptance of school, and at worst in the sense of one's own identity. Each movement is therefore a source of failure—or strength.

Fortunately, and partly because English is so rooted in experience outside school, the resources for new strength are latent in all children and young people. We note particularly a resource that becomes our major concern, in the high school and beyond: the power through language to take on the role of spectator and thus to enter into and share in the work of the mature artist and thinker.

Chapter 3

An analysis of activities in class

THE process of abstraction has characteristic virtues and dangers. It allows us conveniently to collect all the multifarious English activities under four broad headings: on the one hand, talk and drama; on the other, writing and reading. And this is salutary. We are reminded that the essential basis for work in class is simple— though not monolithic. Looking at the two pairs of activities we note that talk is public and arises in the human interaction from which drama springs. By contrast writing and reading are private, solitary operations. But think again: plays become texts, and texts can be enacted and read aloud. In fact, through most of its history literature has meant the public recital rather than the printed text. If the four categories are used at all crudely the dangers of abstraction begin to emerge.

An abstract system is so neat. It invites curriculum guides and textbooks that look exclusively at each activity in turn. It implies a hierarchy of learning, a moving on from the elementary things that a child brings with him to school, like talk and make-believe play, to the more complex. It suggests that some lessons will be for talk, some for drama, some for writing. . . . Insidiously the system begins to lose its original purpose, which was to simplify and organize our notions of complex class activities, and takes on a new role. Its abstract schema may be imposed on the actual lessons themselves. Thus there are today many schools where English is split up into composition periods, language periods, literature periods, with maybe a poetry period too. Even schools that have been critical enough of the heritage model to recognize talk and drama may well set aside fragmented periods for Drama, Speech or Discussion. When this splitting off happens persistently, each activity is likely to become an abstract process divorced from the real purposes of using language. After all, what is written is there to be shared, to be listened to and talked over. And similarly, after a group have acted their improvised play, the response and the talk that follow may well stimulate them to modify their earlier ideas and to write up a script. There is a natural flow from one basic activity to another; more often than not two or three of the four are needed as complementary parts of a single "lesson".

The Seminar's decision to advocate a unitary rather than a fragmented approach to English has important consequences. If in the course of reading some poems with a class, the teacher sees possibilities for acting, or if in the accompanying talk pupils are so seized with the topic that they want to write, then a unitary approach permits the flow from a prepared activity to one relatively unforeseen. Lessons become less preformulated. This is not to reject pre-planning and system: on the contrary, a teacher who is planning flexibly needs to consider beforehand *many* possible avenues that his pupils may discover in the course of a lesson, so that whichever catches their enthusiasm he is aware of its possibilities. The more active the part pupils are given, the more difficult to predict all that they will find and uncover: thus the need for a flexible teaching strategy rather than rigid lesson plans, and for teachers confidently able to move with a class for instance from reading *My Childhood* to discussing old people they know or to acting encounters of youth and age. This question will be discussed more fully in the chapters that follow.

What unifies such varied classroom activities is the theme or aspect of human experience on which work centres. Some of the fundamental "lessons" that pupils learn in English have already been suggested in the extracts quoted from pupils' writing: they learn about the fascination of living things like newts; the permanence and transience of flowers, trees, and people; the sense of loss; and, inevitably, about themselves. As they do so, an important but secondary level of learning arises, learning about keeping a diary, writing a poem, and composition. Our curriculum guides and syllabuses talk a good deal in terms of these secondary abstractions. But we teachers organize the activities in the hope of effecting insight into experience; they are means to an end. When they are not, when "skill" in acting or speaking or writing becomes an end in itself, English loses contact with the humanities and becomes a kind of parlour game. "How to write a good composition" becomes a sophisticated sort of trick that can be achieved without reference to "precious lifeblood". What is the answer? Not to dismiss any discussion of composition at all, but to warn ourselves beforehand of its inevitable limitations.

Talk and drama

These two activities belong together for a number of reasons. Both are found among pre-school children and form the basis for later work in language. Talk underlies all subjects in school. Drama, starting from the simplest representations of experience—the baby pushing four bricks across the floor saying "shu-shu"— diversifies out to include, say, Plato's *Symposium* (recently produced on B.B.C. television) and *A Midsummer Night's Dream* (with echoes of the primitive form). For talk enters into the whole range of human interaction, and drama builds, from that interaction and talk, images of human existence.

Our vision of the place of drama and talk in English depends on a new vision of the classroom. When the dominant means of teaching is the lecturer (and some college and university teachers of English still earn this title), drama and talk are pushed into the background or ignored. In many universities and schools this is still the case today. But there is an alternative vision of teaching as the dialogue of tutor and student (and we may add, the dialogue of "students teaching each other"—Robson): it was an agreed concern at the Seminar to reassert that tradition from primary school to university —to put the round table (Muscatine) in place of the "disappearing dais".

At its simplest, talk arises in doing things together, in making a display, a tape or a film, for example, or perhaps in looking at something together (from rabbits to factory workshops or building sites). Of course, both kinds of talk, and especially the first, arise in many subjects besides English, but it is only recently that even teachers of English have become fully aware of the different roles they may take on in such talk. Let us imagine a class of young school leavers who have sparked off a discussion of their first encounters with work in part-time jobs. Here a teacher can help by noticing and reinforcing a potential change in the level or direction of the discussion, summing up an attitude perhaps, making an issue quite explicit, or calling for an instance when generalizing seems to have lost touch with reality. Learning to do so, without disturbing the tentative informal exploration that good talk becomes, is a matter of awareness and tact. Suppose that one group want to follow up the discussion by making a tape based on their experiences; now the role will vary. Sometimes, when the group is working confidently and constructively, the teacher will pick up the talk as if he was another member of the group, leaving the pupils the initiative and merely nudging them on their way. But if a group stumbles over the complex planning involved or fails to see enough of the possibilities, he may need to take on a different role, trying through discreet questions and comments to develop a framework that will help them on their way. Perhaps he will read them some similar experiences of Paul Morel's from *Sons and Lovers*. Should they decide to visit a factory and observe youngsters like themselves, he may well revert to his role in the first discussion.

Whenever English is based on first-hand experience and real life a teacher needs to look hard at the role he can best fill. Generally the focus of his attention is on the experience and how to elicit a fuller understanding of it. Where, then, does he turn his attention to the *manner* of speaking? Surely with the need for a presentation of findings to a group of classmates, the entire class, or a still larger part of the school community. Effective speech is learnt not in front of audiences who are only to be conjured in the imagination—the dummy run approach—but in preparation for saying something of significance to real audiences. When a class works in groups—on the language of advertisements, say—a simple presentation by each group is natural and inevitable. When the class as a whole have found a theme that inspired them, or produced a radio ballad, this is a natural thing to present in school assembly. In such circumstances a limited conception of what is involved will produce failure; as Alexander Frazier notes, the teacher cannot "settle for judgements made according to such questions as these: Did the speaker stand up straight? Look us in the eye? Make any errors in grammar? Say AH or UR between sentences?" A pupil might "fail" on nearly all these minor points and still successfully challenge his audience to respond to what he had to say. Think of the reports by school journey groups, and the voluntarily prepared appeals for UNICEF Christmas cards: under the pressure of having something worthwhile to say to a school assembly, children and young people are surprisingly well able to address a large group (and even to play on its susceptibilities!) But success at this level is like an iceberg; below, and often ignored, is the confidence developed in class that one has after all things of value to say, experiences to share, with the teacher and with others in the group. In English this talk is a unifying force that knits together the other activities. "It is through . . . talk that children can best find out in exchange with one another what are their responses to an experience, real or symbolic, and help one another to come to terms with it. Such talk does not occur in the classroom, however, without deliberate design; it is most likely when small groups of pupils talk about matters which engage their deepest attention. Nor will children talk in this way unless they feel that their responses and opinions are valued, and this has implications for the teacher's relationship with his pupils. Works of literature enter this talk as voices contributing to the conversation, and the talk in its turn provides a context for literature, which helps the children to take in what the voices have to say" (Barnes).

When talk is so central to English there are obvious dangers in introducing a specialist course in speech. The possibility of more formal presentations developing out of a good deal of informal talk is thereby diminished. The material for those presentations, which arises so naturally in English work of the kind we envisage, is not directly available to a speech specialist and thus the emphasis may fall on "skills" shorn of content. The occasion for speaking to a larger audience may not arise in a speech period. On the other hand it is agreed that weaknesses in teacher education have resulted in some English teachers themselves lacking confidence and facility in public speaking. In an interim situation, therefore, compromises may have to be made: thus it was proposed that between say sixteen and eighteen pupils might be offered a set of options in speech education, including public speaking and dramatics. In the long term, team teaching may offer the best solution, especially when it is so designed that colleagues learn by working with each other. The situation is not dissimilar from that in drama, which, as Albert Kitzhaber remarked, "opens up possibilities . . . and raises problems of teacher preparation . . . that in the U.S. have received almost no attention so far". The implications and possible solution of both these problems will be discussed in a later chapter.

Drama itself arises inevitably from talk: at one moment a pupil is telling the class about stevedores at work; the next he is on his feet, enacting with gesture and movement the poise and grip of the man. "Down he goes on his knees, to lift the big wooden crates. Not the light stuff but the big splintery chunks of wood, held together by long rusty staples. His big brown hairy hands gripping into the fortress of wooden chunks . . ." (Michael, a thirteen-year-old from a low stream, wrote this after such talk.) It is only another step for the class to break into groups exploring manual work of many kinds—at the pitface, on the building site, on the farm—; and then at a pre-arranged signal from the teacher, such as the bang of a tambour, an accident happens, stories begin to develop.

"Drama, then, differs from other talk in three ways: movement and gesture play a larger part in the expression of meaning; a group working together upon an improvisation needs more deliberately and consciously to collaborate . . .; the narrative framework allows for repetition and provides a unity that enables the action more easily to take on symbolic status" (Barnes).

Our everyday experience tells us that talk, gesture and movement work together. In this sense "all effective teaching in the classroom situation is dramatic by its very nature. The relationship within the classroom is a dynamic one; there is a constant interplay between teacher and class, and between members of the class itself." In a group situation, the relationships that are set up develop strong dramatic overtones. Karel Reitz catches exactly this feeling in filming a youth club discussion (run by a teacher) in his documentary *We are the Lambeth Boys*: looking on from outside we see the group as "characters"—in a situation where they all come alive.

Till fairly recently, work in drama has been bedevilled by a (limited) sense of the stage tradition, of theatre not drama. Yet even as these words are written a four-year-old in a red stocking cap stalks past my window, his yellow sword slung on his back. It is there before us all.

"By assuming a role—taking on a stance, setting up a model—a child is trying out a version of himself and his possibilities without committing himself permanently, and as in story-telling or poem-making is both choosing and laying a basis for future choices of personality and values" (Barnes).

The taking on of dramatic roles, the dramatic encounter with new situations and with new possibilities of the self, is not something we *teach* children but something they bring to school for us to help them develop. Their play reminds us—if only we observe—that our verbally dominated college culture takes in only part of life and, carried into school, confuses and even repels children without our verbal confidence. To help pupils encounter life as it is, the complexity of relationships in a group and dynamic situation, there is nothing more direct and simple that we can offer them than drama. "Children will find many ways to tell their stories—what the child can draw and paint he knows. What he can show in bodily movement, he knows—let him tell where he is in the mainstream of life and learning. Listen to the songs he sings . . ." (Wilt). Through the delight of taking a role, of finding new meanings of the body's movements and gestures, young children will come to adapt language as they know it to new roles and levels. And often the language will be the last area in which confidence develops. So "drama opens up to the inarticulate and illiterate that engagement with experience on which literature rests".

Not that one works alone in learning a role. We need to envisage a pair or a group improvising together. For example, "the talk of a class of able thirteen-year-olds began with a printed passage about a quarrel and moved from anecdote to generalizations about anger, its appearance and function; as some of the generalizations were unrealistic, the teacher invited the pupils to quarrel with one another in pairs and then compare what they had observed. This led to further improvisations in which the teacher joined, but before long the class had stopped moving and were talking again at a general level . . ." (Barnes). Drama, like talk, is learning through interaction. The actor may and must find within himself what it is to be angered, hurt, intimidated, ashamed, vindictive . . . but he finds this partly in response to another person. Together they learn to support and confirm each other's discoveries. Because each of us in acting makes public what he knows and can say, others can join in our learning. And the teacher too has the work before him, in progress, open to his sympathetic inspection. Thus he too is positioned to help the work along, to suggest changes of perspective, to focus attention, as the man who observes can.

As drama develops, the learning becomes more complex. Pupils of fourteen to eighteen learn to change and reverse roles, to see the situation from many perspectives, and—in the work of writing scripts —to use the many voices of the "characters" to build within themselves an image of the complexity of the world as they know it. Preceding the scripts and developing through them is a new discipline of interpretation, of seeing more than one way of "reading" a situation. To work on a scene is to realize the complexity of human feeling and attitudes. Thus drama makes explicit the variousness of life, but also acknowledges its elusiveness. The best scripts remind us that "Your good writer is your wide and various man: a character nicely conscious of the elements of personhood excluded by this or that act of writing and ever in a half-rage to allude to them: to hint at characterological riches even where these can't be spent" (Demott).

So, when we eventually come to texts by mature dramatists, the method for exploring their meaning should be fully developed. "When a group of children (or students) is able to re-create script as if it were their own improvisation, this is indeed self-exploration, though with the subtler aid of the dramatist's words. And it is improvisation that can help children to bring to script those aspects of their real and imaginary experience which will enable them to re-create the dramatist's words as if they were their own. If a play is put into the hands of a group of pupils with no more than the instruction to 'act' it, what they will do is likely to show little sign of an imaginative reconstruction of the script in voice and movement unless the class is accustomed to improvisation. And still less valuable is the over-academic approach which assumes the pupils' ability to experience the play and so moves straight from a 'reading' of the text to impersonal literary comment, usually provided by the teacher. (The talk of a group of pupils who are engaged in interpreting a script may be for most of our pupils the most meaningful form of literary criticism.) In sum it is proposed that if a play is to be meaningful to pupils it must be approached in ways that bring the activity closer to improvisation. And this remains true even for work with sixteen- to eighteen-year-olds (and beyond?), though at that stage once the play has been given imaginative life the students can progress to more objective discussion" (Barnes).

"For example," he continues later, "a class of thirteen-year-olds was asked to improvise in pairs a squabble between a man and his supercilious wife who leaves in a huff, to act (alone) a mixture of fear and determination in approaching a growling dog, to fondle and talk to it, and to improvise some other situations closely related to the Prologue of Shaw's *Androcles and the Lion*. When these improvisations had been practised, shown to one another, and talked about, pupils worked in threes upon a short section of the Prologue, acting it with scripts, putting down the scripts and improvising dialogue, watching other groups act, and discussing first the intonations and movements and then by a natural progression the nature of what was being presented. When they finally acted the whole Prologue in groups, this slight and conventional episode came to life because it was filled with perceptions of their own."

In scenes from the mature play, as in much of children's own improvising from ballads and myths, we are strongly conscious of something more in drama than holding up the mirror to nature—the mode of literal presentation of life. From their earliest years, children's simplifications of role and interaction, and the ritual style of their speech, lend themselves to a symbolic presentation of life.

"During the [early] years the typical sources of these symbols tend to be first the home (Mothers and Fathers, Funerals, etc.) and then—especially for boys—to move slowly away and to depend on symbols provided from without, on the one hand from folk tales (Kings and Queens, Witches, etc.) and on the other from the popular media (Cowboys and Indians, Daleks, etc.). What is taken over is, however, little more than the basic situation and some names and catch phrases which identify the roles. To an outsider who happens not to recognize the catch phrases, the play seems formless, repetitive and of little meaning; it is not designed to communicate to outsiders, yet the intensity of its participants testifies to its significance for them. At this stage music can be of great value in generating new patterns of dramatic play. It is only later, perhaps from ten years onwards, that children begin—with adult encouragement—to be able to explore a situation more explicitly, so that their improvised dialogue and actions have public validity. As their power to make public the dramatic symbol increases, new classroom possibilities emerge, perhaps from twelve years onwards. First, it becomes possible to introduce scripts into the dramatic activities: the adult script provides what at an earlier stage is provided by folk-tales or by the popular media, but it does so more explicitly. The teacher should aim to find scenes (or whole plays) which offer as powerful symbols as before, but which through their language give a more sensitive and orderly meaning to the dramatic activity. [Besides well-known scenes from the Mystery cycles and the Elizabethans, we should remember modern work by Arden, Bolt, Brecht, Capek, Frisch, Miller, Obey, Odets, Shaw and others.] Secondly, at a more practical level, it is possible to ask pupils to re-create social situations using the appropriate language. By mid-adolescence the pupil's language abilities have developed far from the largely undifferentiated language of the pre-school years, and he has begun to specialize his language uses according to his purpose and situation. For those adolescents who are deprived of a wide range of social experience, dramatic re-creation of realistic situations may be an important way of developing control of a range of registers. It is here suggested, however, that this should be subordinated to the symbolic function of drama, primarily because drama may be, for many deprived children, the most important creative medium, since it demands less verbal explicitness and is inseparable from expressive movement" (Barnes).

We note that here in drama, as in written English in general, a variety of specialized purposes are emerging. The childish matrix has diversified and by fifteen to eighteen confident pupils may be curious to meet and develop drama in a wide range of modes—how wide we have only recently been reminded in the work of Brecht. Given the development in drama that we envisage, pupils will read the mature dramatist with an appropriate discipline—a discipline that acknowledges the written text not as an overheard dialogue, but as exact cues to sequences of movement and gesture expressive of a particular human interaction. (It is a discipline that most of us in the past conspicuously failed to hear of at the university.) They will read, too, with a fresh enjoyment for all that recalls the elementary forms of drama—from the songs in *Twelfth Night* to the trial in *The Caucasian Chalk Circle*. The battles of Antony and Caesar and all that might escape the literary eye will gain a new visual dimension.

Before this is possible, though, we have to plan for the education of teachers and provision in school. About these the Seminar was quite clear. "We would urge upon training institutions the need to give [intending] teachers experience in drama work . . . in practice rather than simply in theory; and we would see the school English Department itself as an important instrument of training here. It is possible, for example, to combine classes so that the drama 'expert' on a department staff can work alongside his less expert colleagues and in this way can help their training while educating the children. . . . We are concerned about the lack of adequate facilities in many schools for this kind of work, and would urge the widespread conception of an English workshop—equipped with stackable furniture, sound-proofed tape-recording booths, space readily available for movement work, drama rostra etc. The Seminar should go on record as demanding an adequate provision of facilities of this kind to enable the English teacher to do his job."

On both sides of the Atlantic, work is needed to draw together experiences of good drama teaching and of its relationships with all the other activities of English. The problems of self-conscious adolescents and of children who feel in any way threatened by the public nature of drama were considered in detail at the Seminar; some teachers may feel trapped by the same pressures and we should be clear about the best ways to release them. The demand is not for professional actors or producers of school plays: the latter can safely be left to teachers of special interest and expertise—though a taste of classroom drama often in practice leads to a thirst for something more. What is required is an awareness among teachers of English of those moments in a lesson, or in a week's work, when what has been said or read moves naturally out to enactment with movement and gesture.

This demands a knowledge of teaching method, and a detailed sense of the sequence in drama, which moves from the simplest role and schema of events to the more complex, from improvising language and movement to exploring in action the meaning of a script, from being one's own playwright to meeting mature writers. Thus what starts as drama moves into writing and reading. In a developed stage (somewhere between twelve and eighteen) work in drama involves: *improvising* talk appropriate to a vast range of situation and role; *listening and responding* in the fullest sense, while taking a role; *discussing* the approach to a theme, its possibilities, and finally the insights gained; *writing* scripts for one's own group; *reading*, learning and probing the meaning of a text—through private study, talk and enacting.

In this inclusiveness drama is central to English work at every level. Is this surprising when we consider that it is the most direct representation of life (and that implies all life from scientific discovery to internal monologue)? It is naturally therefore a central part of children's play; equally naturally, through television, film and theatre it is *the* form of literature that is common to all people in modern industrial society; it incorporates an immensely flexible mode of language that extends, even in the classical texts, into narration, description, argument, lyric and oration.

"Drama" means doing, acting things out rather than working on them in abstract and in private. When possible it is the truest form of learning, for it puts knowledge and understanding to their test in action. A book is an inadequate medium for the discussion of drama and talk: one cannot present work in progress in all its immediacy. But suppose a film had been made, rather than a book, to report our Seminar's vision of English. Drama and talk would then have been central, with writing and reading in the background somewhere. The medium shapes the message (as with language). This important caveat has two implications. First, work at the centres for curriculum development in English needs to incorporate film and television, radio and sound recording, for otherwise drama and talk will tend to be neglected in discussions there. (B.B.C. television has more than once shown the possibilities of the medium for discussing improvised drama.) Second, the centres themselves need to become English workshops where, at their own level, teachers are encouraged to talk, act, write and give recitals of readings, to sustain and develop their insight into similar work with pupils.

Writing and reading

In moving on to writing and reading we are not moving away from drama and talk but incorporating their discoveries into a new medium with its own special possibilities and, as it grows to independence, its own demands for special varieties of language and gesture. When a class and their teacher use language "to explore their common universe" they become a language community, in which all are learning together as they develop a classroom dialogue that in part can be internalized by each pupil. Just as we take up an overall meaning from a play by internalizing each of the characters and feeling the sum of their relationships, so in class the individual takes up from the discussion of experience what will make sense of his own world. This process of internalizing is developed and extended by writing. To write then is to move from the social and shared work to an opportunity for private and individual work. But the private work takes its meaning from what has gone on before: thus, as we shall see, writing-assignments without a background of discussion and shared experience are unlikely to elicit much response from many children and young people.

This is why the splitting up of English activities and the neglect of talk and drama has had such disastrous effects on writing. While speech is the medium of home and neighbourhood interaction, writing is largely or completely the medium of the school, and the child whose school writing is stultified has little else to draw on. Thus most of us have observed, as Holbrook did in backward classes, pupils whose gossip is full of vitality but whose writing (like that of many a Freshman English course) is felt to be an occasion "for correcting the propriety and accuracy of the language used". We can view it this way: a sense of the social system of writing has so inhibited and overawed many teachers that they have never given a pupil the feeling that what he writes is his own. And yet, paradoxically, while in speaking we may be expected casually to pick up and adopt from others the phrases and attitudes that pass as currency, in writing we work on our own, with our own resources.

It is true that to take what he wants from the currency of classroom discussion is not a simple matter for any pupil. Much depends on the quality of interaction in which writing is rooted. When talk seems to be arriving at answers, and the teacher directs discussion that way, the writing will generally follow an agreed line. This fits well with matters of abstract and logical precision, but rather badly with the stuff of everyday human experience. To encounter this, discussion needs to be probing, exploratory, tentative—seeking to push back the boundaries of an experience rather than draw them tight; thus there is both room and need for individual work in writing. It is as if the teacher brought a magnifying-glass into the classroom. She might show the children her choice of things; or she might show a few transient things like raindrops, say, and leave the glass lying around; or she might give it to the children, suggesting they look for changes in things when they are magnified, and come and tell her about them. In all three cases children have something to talk and write about, but not all offer the same pressure and opportunity for personal exploration.

Let us take the example literally. After she had looked at a rose through the magnifying-glass, this is what Nicola (aged seven) wrote:

When you smell the roses
They smell so lovely
They are so pretty
The rose looks like a fairy dancing in the moonlight.
Skip, hop and jump they go
Sometimes they are red
Sometimes they are pink.
Their little cushion is tucked in the petals.
The petals feel so soft
Like velvet hearts dancing round each other
They curl up together.
At night they go to bed in their warm green homes.
The little yellow thing in the middle looks like a star in the setting sun.

We all have more or less difficulty in breaking away from the customary view of things that society (so usefully) hands on to us through language. It may be that this process is what the first seven lines represent, though without knowing Nicola at that moment, we cannot be sure, since what is cliché for us may be a discovery for a child. But of one thing we can be certain: in the lines that follow there is a new strength, a new investment in the experience of writing, and a correspondingly original and personal vision. At this point, indeed "the writing may be the act of perceiving the shape of experience,—not the evidence that it has [once] been perceived" (Britton). Writing that relates experience and language under this kind of pressure might well be called "imaginative", since, whatever the topic, such writing involves the individual process of drawing from the resources of language whatever (and only what) is necessary to make experience real.

In much conversation and writing "the words we choose (or accept as the best we can find at the moment) may obliterate or slightly obscure or distort fine features of the non-verbal background of thinking. Some people are unaware of this because they speak or write so fluently that thought processes apart from words seem scarcely to occur; the verbal moulds are ready to shape their thinkng from the start. . . . A subtler use of language often consists in breaking and reshaping the more familiar verbal moulds . . . [and at its best] a good deal of speaking and writing involves the effort to be a little more faithful to the non-verbal background of language [in mental functioning] than an over-ready acceptance of ready-made terms and phrases will permit" (Harding: *Experience into Words*). Writing, with its lack of pressure for continuous utterance, perhaps more often permits this effort, and in this respect is most like discussion where we philosophize, pausing perhaps for a minute to mull over an idea. (Thus the famous silences in Wittgenstein's seminars!)

The first factor, then, in helping pupils reach their own decisions in writing rather than take ready-made those of society, is to let exploratory talk precede writing. A second factor is form. It is a common experience that children and young people enjoy free forms. The deliberate introduction of topic sentence method and stanzas is more likely to prevent their having something to say than assist it. Pupils need the opportunity to choose the form that suits them, and this means that for many a lesson when a class are writing enthusiastically there will be a mixed output of poems, dialogues and pieces of prose. This is something to encourage, for it springs from a natural variety in mood, intention and level of insight, and often reveals an intuitive sensitivity in the choice of an appropriate form. Moreover, young children thrive on forms they improvise, like this:

> I wish I liked onions.
> They have a penetrating smell.
> On a plate they look delicious
> Small, curly, like small snails
> In the pan, cristling away
> Oh! I do hope that one day
> I get to like onions.

Simple organic form of this kind is noticeable in several of the examples on other pages. This is not to deny that the confident and mature pupil will seek out forms from the adult writer. There is a fascination in realizing how even a simple stanza will pair and oppose ideas, draw things to a conclusion, check and release the flow of feeling. . . . The form a young writer voluntarily commits himself to "draws out his powers and makes him grasp and penetrate its objections" (Buber). Taken in this spirit it is not a social yoke but a challenge.

The third factor is perhaps the most insidious. It is the teacher—and not the completely insensitive teacher either. Maybe in a fruitful way the presence of an imaginative teacher must often be with pupils as they write. We recall Lawrence's boys writing:

> And one after another rouses
> His face to look at me,
> To ponder very quietly,
> As seeing, he does not see.

But always there is the danger of a closed, behaviourist solution: "by [the teacher's] example and general or specific expressions of approval, children [may] learn at once a style of seeing and feeling, and also a style of writing about what is felt and seen" (Douglas). Yes. And the writing for a time will appear good to us, though somehow less varied and personal. Yet there remains a sense of limitation, a restrictiveness that all of us who care for imaginative uses of language must be concerned about. Of course, there will always be points in a pupil's experience—as in our own—when something is learnt from adopting the stance of a person who impresses and draws us; but that is not the answer. Something has to be noted in the way experience is approached in class, in the teacher's stance as the class share their experience, and in the complex of evaluations that proceed as written work is read out and presented. Is it that "the teacher conveys to young children—by his attitude to poetry and fiction—that he is able to receive and respect significant engagements with experience, on an objective 'third ground' of imaginative effort with words"? (Holbrook). Partly; and partly too in simple talk we may see the right attitude develop when the teacher, instead of capping pupils' stories or coming in as an observer might,

E

lets his excitement at what the last speaker has said betray him into making his own contribution, telling as one of the group how perhaps he watched a huddle of ducklings bob over the ripples on the pond.

In the final resort, the liberation of pupils from the limits of the teacher's vision comes through his growing tentativeness and sensitivity to language, qualities that are most likely to be developed if we teachers are on the look-out for emerging interest and preoccupations in the pupils, not merely in ourselves. When we suggest a topic or broad theme that may help to give structure to their curiosity—the notion of Contrasts, for example—we should be prepared for the class to accept or reject it after discussion. And when the contrast of tame and wild is discussed and written about, we should be prepared for the pupil who discovers, like this one, that the two interpenetrate:

Tame

He came towards me
Not afraid at all
Closer flickering his wings
But although he looked so tame
I knew he was as scared
As I never could, ever be
And as he spread his wings
He chirped No No Goodbye.

A teacher of English, one could well say, spends his time in his better hours discovering *through* his pupils. This is not hyperbole. It follows inevitably if we accept personal experience as the vital core of English work. Then "good creative work can only be spontaneous, and the teacher works best when he works with opportunities as they arise. Why children decide to take *hate* one week and *flowers* the next as themes is unpredictable, but it is necessary to important dynamics of their exploration of life to do so; and the creative teacher must follow, enlarge, and deepen" (Holbrook).

Of course, the teacher at the same time should have a wider perspective and a sense of overall purpose, which he uses not only to help him nudge pupils in a particular direction but also to sharpen his awareness of needs they obscurely indicate. Thus in writing we can follow growth along at least two dimensions. From their earliest days children enjoy shaping their world through the simplifying order of fictions, playing Red Riding Hood to the Wolfs of their environment, or tumbling the beanstalk world of adults down to their own (proper) level. "A child's stories are often richly ambiguous —like the tales he likes to hear and read. They may be his way of thinking and managing experience" (Moffett). The "poetic, meta-phoric, intuitive understanding" gained in this way "*is* a form of knowledge although it cannot be objectively measured" (Hoggart). Therefore, as pupils mature we want them to continue to use and develop symbolic representations of this kind—"to organize the material of their own experience into a model—or image—which will have validity in organizing diverse and different experiences".

Opposed to this symbolic mode of representation, interacting and interpenetrating, will be writing of a different level, that of literal representation. These are poles to a continuum, and the poem "Tame" suggests a place where closeness of sensory observation (the literal) interacts with a feeling that what is observed represents also something inside ourselves (the symbolic). Hopkins' notebooks sometimes take up the same process at a mature level.

In the early years, the strength of literal representation is often in the sensory world. Here for example is a ten-year-old drawing on observations at the swimming baths:

At the Baths.

I will always remember the first time I went to the baths. As I entered through the doors I could hear distant hollow noises coming from the baths. It gave me a queer feeling inside me. The hollow noises seemed to echo, muffled and dull, over the bath. In the locker room the noise was muffled and distant. In the water the noise was louder than ever. The harsh crisp sound of someone jumping in shattered the echoing noise. Then the shrill clear sound of the whistle broke the noise and everyone hurried off chattering quietly. The noise seemed to be trapped inside the baths and couldn't get out. It seemed to bounce off the water up to the ceiling and then bounce back to the water again.

Already there is a surprising complexity of explicitness and sugges-tiveness in the language: we are not so far from Hopkins' inscapes. But psychological observation of a similar explicitness probably has to wait until adolescence, starting as the sensory level does with egocentric observation, and gradually working out. Consider, for example, the growth between the following two pieces, one by a ten-year-old boy, the other by a girl of fourteen. It is knowledge of this kind that the teacher of English must be able to draw on, applying it not to the class but to the individual pupil.

"Oh Ian do something for heavens sake?
What
Go for a ride on your bike.
Got a puncture.
Well go and day dream then.
That's a good idea. I daydream about things like
         designing boats and go-karts and things like that.
Quarter of an hour later.
Ian will you help me plant these flowers.
I don't want to.
I don't know. Not long ago you were frantic for something to do.
I found something to do.
No you haven't you're just sitting there. Trouble with you you're just
         plain lazy.
But I . . .
Oh!! What a life.

                                        *   *   *

I was in trouble again; this time for being saucy to my grandmother. I hadn't thought I was being cheeky but adults seem to see things in a different light. My tongue is always getting me into trouble. It all began, the trouble this evening, when I was figeting in an arm chair, I was not interested in the play my parents were watching. I made critical remarks and was sharply told, "We're listening to the play, not to you." I got up and walked towards the door, "Where are you going?" It was always the same wherever I went I was asked the same question. Why couldn't they leave me alone? I felt a surge of resentment. I came back and stood in front of the fireplace. I was then told gruffly, "You're blocking Nanny's view."

    "If she can't see, she should say so and not wait for someone else to do it." There! I had said it, it just slipped out before I knew it. My mother sat forward in her chair. Nobody was looking at the television now, all eyes were focussed on me. They were all eyeing me with dislike, probably thinking what a horrid girl I was. I was thinking the same about myself. If only I could take those words back, but I couldn't.

    "Go to bed," said my father sternly.

"But it's only just gone ten," I said rebelliously.

"Go to bed," said my father, the tone of his voice developing into a shout. I went to the door, without turning I said "goodnight" to them, I usually kissed them, but not tonight. I felt the tears well up inside me, my nose tingling as I tried hard to fight back the tears.

"Haven't we got names," said my father.

"Goodnight Nan, goodnight Dad, goodnight Mum," I said shortly as if reading a list. Then I went from the room, banging the door behind me.

In the bedroom I sat on the edge of my bed, shivering in the dark. I wanted to have a good cry but the tears would not come. I turned my bedside lamp on and got into bed. With a faint smile I remembered I had some sweets under my pillow. Things to eat always gave me comfort when I was in trouble, I said my prayers, this usually comforted me, but at that moment I felt that He would not want to listen to a horrid girl like me. My mother had often said "Never let the sun go down on your anger". But I was too proud to go and apologize so I went to sleep unsettled and I knew tomorrow would start badly too. I sighed, hardly a day went by without having an argument. "Oh God, please make me less argumentative and help me curb my quick temper and my tongue."

At both levels, the sensory and the psychological, there are common qualities that we look for in literal representations: "shrewdness of observation . . . fidelity to experience . . . the sort of truthfulness which is born out of interest and personal involvement . . . these things matter most and are the first things for us to look for" (J. H. Walsh). Part of our work in written English, then, is to foster the kind of looking and the kind of talk and writing that direct observation of experience demands. We do so, not in the detached systematic way of a scientist, but by watching for, and even helping to provide, moments when such experiences are of personal importance to pupils. For it is their involvement in the experience that will draw them into writing.

Admittedly, we can offer increasing help in general and in detail as the representation moves towards the literal pole. Primary teachers will take pupils into the woods, encouraging them to feel and smell the bark of trees, to look at the fungi, to collect the autumn leaves . . . and secondary teachers go out with cameras and sketch-pads to look at the men working on bulldozers and cranes, the new concrete skyscrapers, or to stare through grated windows at children pushing prams in the alleys of black tenements. On their way, and maybe back in class, they talk with groups and groups talk together, sharing and probing—to see more and get it clearer—so that later they may build together, through writing, painting, photographs . . . a report of what they found. But at the same time, in the same situations and "lessons", we leave room for the symbolic representation of experience to emerge if it will.

Helping on the symbolic level is a more complex business. There ought to be firm roots, as we have seen, in drama and in the excited response of children who take up the figures of fairy-tale and myth, improvising for themselves stories that will satisfy their partly perceived wishes and fears. (The poem or story that goes home to pupils will continue to strike up its echoes and this redoubles the need, when we read to pupils, to include the best but to draw on it selectively—see p. 65). But though much of symbolic writing is unpremeditated, we shall often meet classes without these roots, for whom it is all uncharted territory. How can we help *them* to reach the confidence and the awareness together? There are simple ways to start: thus, music, paintings, photographs, bizarre objects and complex natural forms (like shells) are just a few of the kinds of stimulus that might be offered in the initial stages. Of course, while people do create to order, "they may flop badly at times; individuals may dry up, or fail. These failures are important and must be endured. (How much does any author burn or throw away!)" (Holbrook).

Nevertheless, there is already a repertoire of initial experiences that have been tried out with considerable response: Bax, *Tintagel*; Boulez, *Le Marteau sans Metre*; Debussy, *Jeux*; De Falla, *El Amor Brujo*; the photographs of *The Family of Man* and work by Capa, Cartier-Bresson, Mayne, Paul Nash and Shahn; paintings by Van Gogh, Toulouse Lautrec, Sutherland, Munch, Rowlandson and the Impressionists. Looking or listening with the concentration that works such as these elicit will often liberate an unsuspected store of imaginative ideas, trapped till then at unconscious levels.

There is, unfortunately, a danger of work never reaching beyond this stage, of a cosy satisfaction on the teacher and pupils' part that "creative work" has been done for this week, thank you very much. The more restricted the outlook of a school or college on English teaching, the more it will tend to isolate and shelve "creativity",

* See p. 53 *The Secret Places*, David Holbrook.

which thus becomes a political word calculated to muddy not to clarify.

Perhaps it is more useful for this reason to speak of *imaginative* use of language (over a wide range) in the terms that Harding has helped to clarify in his discussion (p. 46) of the way words relate to the non-verbal background. Then we can look on the literal-symbolic poles as one dimension in all such imaginative work, with poetry keeping towards the symbolic end and prose generally favouring the literal. As children mature we seem to observe a further dimension developing, that of sensory-psychological observation; here the two categories are more likely to overlap perhaps. Both dimensions vary in the degree of explicitness of meaning. Using this framework, we should say that "creative" is sometimes confined to the poetic domain as against the literal; however, a growing sense of the importance of imaginative activity in even the most literal uses of language has give "creative" a wider implication.

A further confusion has arisen through the fairly recent recognition that imaginative writing, especially the more symbolic, may help all children to compose disorder in their inner world; thus the word "creative" has come to be applied rather exclusively to such self-enhancing work. There are dangers here. Feelings of disorder in our inner selves frequently relate to a sense of disorder in the world at large. Indeed it is natural for "outer" and "inner" to overlap. The eighteen-year-old writer of the following poem, for instance, is surely protesting against something more than his external environment.

Domestic Nature

Commons are despicable things.
Like zoos or pekinese or a budgie's clipped wings,
Or the most abhorrent botanical garden
Where they instal, quite without pardon,
Hard things like railings and bird-baths,
And stone steps and coquettish concrete paths.

But a common I detest most of all.
Its tame trees, its quaintly-rooted paths are gall
To me. With undergrowth listless, shabby,
The whole seems limp and flabby—
Like a middle-aged business-man

Whose body rots as unjust serving-man
To a conceited brain. In this false
Nature, as wild and free as a waltz
We comatose humans stroll smugly,
Murmur "Delightful!" It should be "Ugly!"
And where we blindly pass the boy-smooth bough,
We should weep and remember how;
For we have forgotten how to live.

Poems such as this raise the issue of social circumstances that deeply affect our inner selves. They work by literal as well as symbolic representation, making demands on intellect as much as feeling. They question experience, and to do them justice we have to assess their truthfulness to the outer world as well as the inner.

Of course, if Harding is right about the process of getting "experience into words", then this implies a challenge to teachers in many other subjects beside English to work along with us to see that language is shaped to fit the non-verbal background of thinking, not allowed to distort it through the acceptance of ready-made forms—such as the textbook, the teacher's notes, the unnecessary jargon and fossilized forms of utterance. But it also serves to remind ourselves that we teachers of English must leave room for the level of representation to vary, and when we talk about *personal* experience, must recognize the enormous range of curiosities (leading out into other subjects) that this implies.

The fact is that the English specialist is often tempted to restrict himself to looking at life through fictions—quite forgetting that one can also look at people and situations direct. Those who succumb will dismiss as "sociology" an interest in the life of the city or the countryside. They forget the steady pressure on the writer himself to get out into the light of *things* and bring to all the concerns of common life a heart that watches and receives. If an interest in literature is to inform and modify our encounter with life itself, the teacher must bring into a vivid relationship life as it is enacted and life as it is represented. For some of us this means a readiness to go outside the classroom walls, to meet people, observe them, and work with them, so that we and our pupils can draw from their experience and understanding. For all it must imply at least a readiness to help pupils explore aspects of their immediate lives with the same insight we expect of their fictional representations. Indeed, any failure on our part to bring these processes together means a failure to take adequate account even of literature itself. "Why do men (the child as well as the poet) improvise upon their representations of the world? Basically because we never cease to long for more lives than the one we have . . ." (Britton). Now, we may read a dual character into that longing. In children's drama and stories, as in adult fantasies, we often observe play with representational worlds in order to make them fit more closely to needs and desires that may be only partly conscious. Pursued exclusively this becomes escapism. On the other hand, we "long for more lives" when, despite the richness of our present choice, we sense, regret and celebrate (even) the selves we might have been, or struggle to recognize in ourselves elements we would like to ignore. Such activity is life-enhancing and life-directed. It involves the effort to find in experience more than we thought we knew, or valued. Such an effort is inevitably "imaginative" in our present sense. That is why the work of literary man is related to all work (whatever the subject) where language is used to "structure" experience, bringing it into new order, and taking account of new elements.

With this in mind a wide definition of literature was used throughout the Seminar. Thus, when pupil's stories and poems, though necessarily private activities, re-emerge as experience to be shared and talked over with teachers and classmates, they become the literature of the classroom. The acceptance of pupils' work as embryonic literature carried important implications. It reminds us of the need to encourage each pupil "through making discoveries about himself and about people in general to 'make small steps towards maturity' ". Further, in so far as a pupil succeeds, he has something of value to offer others in the class, and thus "he has a right to expect from his audience (including us) a reply to what he has said. Any criticism of language must be introduced very delicately. . . . The tacit presentation of alternatives is preferable."

In the same way, adult literature *earns* itself the right to a hearing in the dialogue of the classroom. Beginning from readings aloud (as if the class overheard) it wins over pupils to private reading, though it never loses that potential public character. When we read to ourselves effectively we make these voices come alive as part of ourselves: they tell us of experience as they know it—we accept in so far as this helps us to make sense of our experience. Literature has no existence "out there"; the writer's sequences of signs take life from within us, from the personal experiences that we as readers draw on and bring to them.

"As often used, 'work of art' suggests the existence of something quite wholly outside the perceiver, existing in ineluctable perfection and subject to only the most partial and inadequate approach, rather like Henry James' mind. . . . We want to suggest that works of art are by no means so separate from us human perceivers" (Douglas). There is no short cut then to each pupil learning to read for himself. Even a presented reading or a play has to be taken up by each individual in the audience out of his sense that the pattern and quality of the experience is a matter of inner satisfaction and enjoyment. So whenever a group read together we can reckon on a variety of satisfactions developing, according to the level of investment each pupil has made in his response.

On different occasions we all invest more or less of ourselves in reading, satisfying as we do more or less of our personality, and, when we feel disposed to put in a good deal, becoming dissatisfied with the mediocre story we had passed the time with before. Thus, sometimes we seek little more from literature than the fun of a play world: "There was an old woman who swallowed a bird. How absurd!" Often these are times for sharing the experience, for chanting chorus (Ground Hog!), bouncing on mother's knee, clapping and the chuckling. (Modern folk-singers, bad as well as good, are reminding us that this chanting, clapping and sharing is a pleasure to prolong into maturer years.) At other times we anticipate satisfaction in the pattern of events, whether ghoulish ("I'm on your one step") or humorous maybe ("Seven foolish fishermen"). And it pays to remember that to a young audience, *Hamlet* is rightly a "What next?" story, while for many a sophisticated adult the detective thriller works in the same vein, and generally offers in the end as safe a world to return to as "Jack and the Beanstalk". Another pleasure we've all enjoyed is to play, as we read, the role of the hero.

Many of the great *texts* become *experiences* such as these in reading. But taken at the right moment they beckon us further, if we have the energy, the human experience, and the felt need to meet their demands. Then we look to literature to bring order and control to our world, and perhaps to offer an encounter with difficult areas of experience without exacting from us the full price. For on the one hand, literature is a world of "supposing . . .; as if . . .". On the other hand, we know that we "accept and reject [stories] because we are required to love, fear, tolerate, judge, be moved by, sympathize, recognize, organize, admit. . . . We should recognize that narrative covers many modes of experience and offers an area for the exercise, testing and control of our imaginative capacities to tolerate ourselves and the outside world" (Hardy).

In reading literature at our highest levels we come closest to the ebb and flow of everyday human activity. The "work" becomes a "virtual experience" (Langer). The move through to those levels is a process we can affect only indirectly, however good our teaching. "Progress lies in being able to perceive more and more complex patterns of events, in picking up clues more widely separated, and more diverse in character, and in finding satisfaction in patterns of events less directly related to our expectations, and more particularly, our desires; at the same time it lies in perceiving the form also of the varying relationships between elements in the story and reality, as increasingly we come to know that commodity" (Britton).

So we may bluntly point out to pupils or delicately elicit from them parts of the pattern, we may talk over relationships of the story with reality, but we cannot do the work for our pupils!—to *feel* those relationships as one is carried through the experience and be deeply involved in it is a different matter from recognizing them at a cool distance away.

A virtual experience is not merely something that passes before our eyes, as it were. In making things real, language cannot help but give them value and meaning (through things as simple as the order chosen for events, or the set of roles offered). Thus literature invites us into ways of evaluating aspects of life *as* we experience them. But when we experience life through literature, we do so in the role of spectator and not participant. This is why the reader can share with the author a satisfaction "that has something in common with the satisfaction he feels, not so much in having an experience as in looking back on an experience he has had". We see this at the classroom level: Hilda begins her story about being in trouble again (p. 50), still partly in the role of participant, but later she moves to a greater distance, seeing not only others but herself more dispassionately, and ends by feeling not shame but a rueful awareness of herself as she is. As she moves into the role of spectator, is there not perhaps a "more widely comprehensive" evaluation, as Harding suggests? (p. 29).

During the Seminar, our sense of the role of spectator came to define the term "literature" in our discussions. "Though our central attention was for literature in the ordinary sense we found it impossible to separate this sharply from the other stories, films, or TV plays, or from pupils' own personal writing or spoken narrative. In all of these the pupil contemplates represented events in the role of spectator, not for the sake of active intervention. But since his response includes in some degree accepting or rejecting the values and emotional attitudes which the narrative implicitly offers as appropriate, it will influence, perhaps greatly influence, his future appraisals of behaviour and feeling".

Literature and the teacher's intervention

While the Seminar was united in the essential value of literary experience as sketched in the last few pages, it was full of doubt and dismay about prevailing approaches to the teaching of literature, not only at school level. So many seemed in the process to sap the central enjoyment and satisfaction of the act of reading and responding. There is a widespread and self-defeating refusal on both sides of the Atlantic to see that literature cannot be "taught" by a direct approach, and that the teacher who weighs in with talk or lecture is more likely to kill a personal response than to support and develop it. We are all tempted into doing so, of course. Then "it is all too easy for the immature student, feeling his own responses to be unacceptable, to disown them and profess instead the opinions of the respected critics. And to many teachers, with their eyes on what may rightly go on in other parts of the the curriculum, this looks like good teaching. It may, of course, be the best kind of preparation for an ill-conceived examination, and this may be the real root of the trouble" (Britton). "Pupils—and teachers—need to be encouraged to trust their own responses and not the reverse: it may be a slow business, but these are the inescapable limitations under which we work." Our adult, committed position testifies—or should do—to the many occasions when we have felt what the writer offered "carried alive into the heart by passion". To assume, in children or even in most university students, an equal or similar background of response, for what may well be a first reading of a text, is ridiculous.

Nor is it the case that talk is the appropriate and only testimony to the power of literature. Have we not all known the occasion when the best comment was silence—not a dead silence, but the shared silence of reflection and quiet brooding over what has moved us deeply. A reading aloud of Lawrence's *Odour of Chrysanthemums*, say, is probably going to involve too big an investment of ourselves for any of us in the group to want to talk immediately.

When talk does arise, at its best it springs from the pupils. It may be quite primitive: "That's me!" said a college student, listening to a reading about Clavinger in *Catch 22*. "Are we still at that stage?" was his friend's reply. What would ours be? *"That's me* has two components, and our aim is to move dynamically from the *me* of personal identification to the *that* of the poem or the object in the poem. The discipline lies in the attention to the *that*, and it should be made plain that there is no real dichotomy here, but a natural movement from subject to object and back again. The *That's me* may reveal a very partial and too selective attention to the work, but the teacher will get nowhere in the attempt to make the work meaningful if he does not begin with the *me*. And this kind of identifying is often more interesting than it looks. A middle-aged schoolmaster (university student) who said 'I am Bobadil' was not just being confessional, for he proceeded to look around and say that everyone else was too, and the discussion of the *that* was a discussion of the humanness of Jonson which moved miles away from autobiographical chat. But the particularized response should be primary. There will be movement round the many people in the class, and a restrained and thoughtful sharing of personal, incomplete, and implicit response which can lead back to the particular work, and to repeated sensitive readings. The reference to life is not purely illustrative but confirms the affective experience of literature, and is of course its foundation" (Hardy).

We must constantly remind ourselves that "the principle of

organization of a critical statement is cognitive; that of a work of literature is, in the final analysis, affective." For this reason "*study* of literature is an ambiguous and even deceiving term, which often deflects the energies of teachers from what many of them now consider to be their primary concern. The term suggests, perhaps necessarily, that, in the classroom experience with literary works, pupils and teachers should be seeking regularities and similarities, treating works as data or the source of data for establishing or testing general statements about classes of literary works, their parts, their authors, or the circumstances of their composition; or should be composing rather closed formulations of the probable causes in works of assorted effects in readers." On the other hand, "*response* is a word that reminds the teacher that the experience of art is a thing of our making, an activity in which we are our own interpretative artist. The dryness of schematic analysis of imagery, symbols, myth, structural relations *et al.* should be avoided passionately at school and often at college. It is literature, not literary criticism, which is the subject. It is vividly plain that it is much easier to teach literary criticism than to teach literature, just as it is much easier to teach children to write according to abstract models of correctness than it is to teach them to use their own voices."*

The essential talk that springs from literature is talk about experience—as *we* know it, as *he* sees it (correcting our partiality and his; exploring the fullness of his vision, and ours). Conversely, only in a classroom where talk explores experience is literature drawn into the dialogue—otherwise it has no place. The demand for interpretation—was it this or that he meant?—arises in the course of such talk: otherwise it is a dead hand.

Interpretation implies the desire to read something as it was readily intended, so the demand for it arises most naturally and properly in drama, in choral readings, in the preparation of tape recordings and live recitals. A younger group, for instance, working on *A Midsummer Night's Dream*—I, ii, may wonder what to make of that awkward sentence of Quince's beginning "Here is a scroll . . ."; may see several possible ways of taking Flute's "What is Thisby, a wandering knight?"; may not tumble immediately to Quince's intentions in saying Pyramus is a sweet-faced man—and so on. After

* Response to Literature, N.C.T.E., 1968.

trying these out, their final decisions may well be intuitive, but none the less they can imply subtle awareness of pomp and ceremony, of identifications and daydreams, of soothing flattery. Interpretation however implicit should mean bringing our living experience to bear. Sometimes, it is not so much the line as the whole situation that demands this. If we look at Portia before the assassination (in *Julius Caesar*—II, iv), we see in part what it is for a woman to suffer while the man acts; a group would do well to improvise this scene, to engage for themselves in the struggle to contain oneself, passive in the moment of crisis. It is a beautiful scene for what is not said, but implied. Without an inner awareness of this, the lines mean little. But as they consider how Calphurnia too feared for her husband (with an irony characteristic of the play) a maturer group will want to talk about the particular way that Portia, Cato's daughter, responds.

When we interpret in action, there is less danger of explication becoming an end in itself, or a disconnected, rational appraisal of what has never been personally felt. Implicit expression of meaning will often be the inevitable starting point, especially in such puzzling yet fascinating choric poems as Eliot's *Triumphal March*. A desk analysis of this poem can so easily stunt the delicate, intuitive understandings to be reached through readings in which contrasts of rhythm and changes of register and tone are savoured. Talk will almost certainly be needed to draw together personal experiences (of marches pupils have watched, joined in, seen on film or television): stories about Armistice Day celebrations, recollections—perhaps from *Claudius the God*—of the Roman ceremony, images of the entry into Jerusalem, all have a relevance. Reading such a poem manifestly cannot be a once-for-all experience, will at best be an activity to return to. If the *need* for knowledge is felt, then pupils themselves have time to collect photographs, texts, and parents' impressions from the Fascist marches of the thirties. Another kind of knowledge will come if the class improvise in drama on some of the themes they feel to be underlying.

Even with mature young men and women, the tentativeness of this approach is valid. "As teachers we should remember how long it takes even to respond to poems of our own choice, how often we are quite naturally numb to parts or wholes as we encounter literature.

... In some circumstances early or broad formulation is particularly inappropriate (even at university). When should the teacher try especially hard to sit back, relax, and shut up, to expose fragments elicit fragments, pass on, be superficial? When the student is responding to something very distant in time or convention—say Spenser, or eighteenth-century verse, or Scott—then formulation should wait: empathy is not going to come easily (if at all) and students should not be made to feel that they are aesthetic cripples if they simply do not respond. A toleration of the selective or superficial response may really be a way in. Recognizing the response implicit in an emphasis that looks odd, or hostile, is an important action of the teacher's sensibility.

"It may be hard to move from the *that* to the *me* in reading Scott, but there are those other cases in which it is hard to separate the subject and object, as in an emotionally or sensationally confusing first encounter with something very raw or unaesthetic or powerful (or all three), say Baldwin or Donne or Lawrence. Or there will be the difficulty of something very unlike earlier experiences, art which bursts expectations and makes the identification of the *that* very hard: Beckett would be the adult instance, any teacher will fill in the examples at school level. And there are those works to which we have an over-acculturated response which keeps the *me* miles away from the *that*: how hard it is to take in the fantasy in *Jane Eyre*, or Paul Dombey, or authorial address to the reader, inhibited as we may be at various ages by current attitudes to 'objectivity', 'maturity', 'sentimentality' and dramatic conventions of narrative" (Hardy).

Rather than support the current school trend to explicit analysis that attempts to be "exhaustive" and yet turns out to be largely cognitive, we would stress the need for reading together and acting out, with maturer pupils presenting considered readings of work they want to introduce, and teachers making room for an enjoyable return to works that excited tentative exploration in earlier readings. Remember how often young children will ask for the same story again and again; cannot our teaching build on and add to the store of such experience, so that a poetry anthology, let us say, becomes a genuine "golden treasury" on which a class delights to draw. (And we are fortunate to have such anthologies in schools today, after many dry years in Britain.)

Are there no occasions, it may be asked, when interpretative discussion in school starts from the teacher? Yes, there are. When we read aloud *The Silver Sword*, perhaps, we leave the room for experience to be taken up and probed a little—throwing out, as the story pauses, an enabling comment or question that briefly offers a child the way in to "Yes, he's a funny boy that Jan. Look at the way . . ." Between the ages of twelve and eighteen such interpretative discussions, starting from the pupils, will become more searching and draw in more general perceptions. How far this depends on direct intervention by the teacher is a different question: undoubtedly some members of the Seminar felt it a natural thing to expect and introduce interpretative discussion among older age-groups, but in the main discussions of response to literature the emphasis was largely on when *not* to push for interpretation. Here, for example, are a small group of thirteen-year-olds discussing with the teacher Lawrence's poem "*Last lesson of the afternoon*". This extract comes from the middle of twenty minutes' talk.

Teacher: "I will not waste my soul and my strength for this, What do I care if they do amiss."

Do you think he should?—care?

Anna: Yes.

Teacher: Why?

Heather: They might have . . . sort of . . . might have never . . . the children might never have cared and it may have sort of been years since they cared·about their work and so it's not worth doing anything about it because it's too late.

Deborah: He should not care about whether they are good at English or not but he should care whether he is being a good teacher, he should care whether they . . . he should measure what they do by whether he thinks of himself as a good teacher. He should set his standard according to their work.

Teacher: He says, "What does it matter to me that they can write a description of a dog or if they can't".

Deb: It doesn't, it should matter to his conscience that he is being a good teacher.

Anna: Oh yes, he . . . he . . . he thinks he's a good teacher but he's not a good teacher in the sense maybe the school wants him to be and he's not a good teacher for those children. He wants to be a more Summerhillish sort of teacher. "You must do so and so, you must write a description of

F

a dog because it's on the English syllabus": he doesn't think this is important.

Teacher: I don't know why you want to say he wants to be a Summerhillish sort of teacher.

Anna: Not so sort . . . not so sort of strict and so . . .

Deb: Not conventional.

Richard: He doesn't want to use punishments, etc. etc.

Anna: But his school do.

Teacher: I suppose that's a fair sort of inference.

Rich: And he finds difficulty in getting the fact across to his pupils.

Teacher: Well look, what do you think a description of a dog is meant to represent?

Deb: The sort of useless thing that it would say.

Anna: The useless things they have in English books.

Teacher: Such as?

Deb: Those little books which are absolutely no good. Like in my Junior School, it was called "Focus on," and you used to have a passage and then lots of questions about it.

Anna: And they were questions you could sort of . . . you know . . .

Heath: You copy the answer . . .

Much is still implicit; given a guiding comment from the teacher, the group work to make some things more explicit, and doing so takes them out to common points of reference like the experimental school, Summerhill, or the textbooks they had between the ages of seven and eleven. Their sense that they have something to say—to tell the interested adult—makes them respond positively to a comment like "I don't know why you want to say . . ." The central issue in this poem is perhaps the harshness with which school and pupils are rejected: with the teacher's help they are beginning to understand and evaluate this feeling.

A teacher will sometimes intervene in a rather different way to avoid an audience starting from cold. Poems, for instance, need not always come out of the blue. Asked at the Seminar how he would take Hardy's poem "The man he killed", Ben Demott replied that he might start by discussing with a class the times when they had encountered older strangers (hitch-hiking, maybe), and lead the discussion towards the difficulties of starting a conversation, and the occasions when an older man wants to put over a big experience (sex, marriage, comradeship) and stumbles maybe into a phoney vein. Among talk of such encounters he would read the verses and ask what ring of truth or falsehood they had. Whether a poem requires a context is a matter for decision in each particular lesson— not a general rule. What we can say confidently is that talk which draws on personal experiences in the role of spectator inevitably creates at some point the context for a poem or story that confirms and extends some of our feelings and apprehensions; and, conversely, a poem or story that meets the experience of the class will raise talk in a variety of directions.

The *writing* that springs from literature takes us in two directions: outwards into our own shaping of experience, tapped and activated by our reading—and that is the usual direction—or in towards the writer's experience, sifting and savouring the thing for itself—and that is rarer. But sometimes a disagreement or an uncertainty or another cause will naturally prompt a maturer pupil to write from both impulses.

Preoccupied as we often are with critical "assignments", we sometimes fail to notice the tributes that come unsought when a work has genuinely moved a pupil, yet this is the best kind of commentary. Here is a poem by a ten year-old:

Luring a mortal

Come come to the golden sands
   Come dance with immortal beings,
      Hear with me the gentle lapping of the waves,
      And while we dance,
         The gulls will sing praises to our words.

We'll dance together
   By the shimmering moonlight
      Oh mortal men come with me
         Come come to the golden sands
         Come dance mortal men.

This was written during a morning when children could choose their own activities; it is not teacher-sponsored. It comes in the context of much writing that has a genuinely personal voice. Such a poem then is derivative in the best possible way, taking up an adult stance for its delight and improvising from it, as all children do in dramatic play. We can see it as a special kind of appreciative criticism of Arnold's

Forsaken Merman. Such indirect criticism may remain the most fruitful and natural, well into mature years; it is our characteristic response to the people we admire and would emulate. The danger in the past has come from teachers who would recognize only such writing as good, and who failed to see it as a special departure from a young writer's own unique voice. As a result few of their pupils realized one could do more than imitate adults. To emulate became to ape.

Direct appreciative criticism will indeed emerge very early, but not everyone will write it—written criticism of this kind requires a special commitment. In talk appreciation develops from the "handing back" of all pupils' work. As pieces are read to the class, the teacher encourages a shared enjoyment to be expressed, at first perhaps by saying nothing more than "Did you like that?" when he knows there will be a chorus of "Yes", but gradually beginning to follow up and probe— "Did you feel any movement or dancing as you listened to LURING A MORTAL?"—"When it says LURING what does that suggest to you now?"—or just "Have any of the lines you liked stuck in your mind?—which?" Someone says it is like the Sirens singing to Odysseus, and so connections begin to be made out from one pupil's imaginative world to that of the whole class or group.

The writing of appreciative criticism suggests a special desire to work, say, on a poem that has puzzled or drawn the student, or that he has been delighted to discover a new world through, or even that he suspects, despite its popularity. Though the best of such writing draws on more cognitive awareness, it still keeps its tentativeness, and leaves room for connections with personal experience (something too often stamped out by examination pressures). Rather than the dryness of the scholar, it should carry the life and the weight of felt experience in, say, Dr. Johnson's outburst on Falstaff.

Beyond the "English" lesson

So far we have looked at the ways in which these four central activities—talk, drama, reading and writing—enter into the English lesson. Obviously they are also going to enter into work in many other subjects. In fact, using language to operate on experience is characteristic of most academic subjects (at their best), and this involves learning to use language in new ways, and with new variety, as pupils encounter the earlier stages of each subject discipline. Thus, even so-called "practical" subjects, like the crafts, may incorporate a good deal of planning and thinking over, some of it verbalized, some visual (in diagrams and sketches): anyone who has watched a group of boys designing and making something like a go-kart would acknowledge the complexity and value of the relationship between language and "practical" activity. In scientific disciplines too the preliminary observations, the exact framing of hypotheses (and the choice between them), and the elaboration of verifying experiments, all involve language. Such language operates at several levels of abstraction, from the simplest one of playing a role in the selection of relevant material from the mass of all that is observed, to the complex levels that permit a critical awareness of the conceptual framework to which the hypothesis relates.

"It is impossible to teach any subject without teaching English" said the Newbolt Report in 1919; unfortunately this general awareness has led to very little discussion of the precise ways in which such teaching goes on. We are just beginning to realize how other subject specialists help or hinder the build-up of special varieties and strategies in language, and how appropriate linguistic forms enable pupils to raise and to answer the kind of questions specific to each subject. At present "each school subject seems to operate within its own sub-language encrusted with linguistic conventions, some of which still serve a useful purpose, some of which do not. School textbooks frequently show us these sub-languages at their worst. ... The verbalization of concepts within different subjects has a complex history; it is probably not a simple matter of perfectly evolved language that embodies one kind of rational thought. The models that we look at are social institutions and the differences between say the language of geology and the language of history must be in part due to the different history of these two subjects. My feeling is that the difficulty students face is not simply the difficulty of a certain level of conceptualization but also of more hidden features. In all events we should set about distinguishing between the linguistic-conventional and the linguistic-intellectual, so that we can understand that traditional formulations are not sacrosanct. (Is there only one possible statement of Boyle's Law?)" (H. Rosen).

Subject specialists for the most part are working in language by the light of folk linguistics. This accounts for the common belief that attention to language is a matter for the English lesson, not for Chemistry, say. The non-English specialist, that is, refuses to consider whether the language of his subject may be "so intimately bound up with the specific materials and operations of that subject that the two must be taught together". Safe in his illusions such a teacher repeats in his teaching all the mistakes we have made in English: treating making notes on X as a skill, feeding in vocabulary, drilling in structures (like the impersonal), perhaps even dictating the lot and having it learnt by heart. Here, for example, is a writer for the Science Masters' Association of Great Britain discussing how to help "weaker" pupils describe their observations:

> It would be best to give the class a suggested account—too quickly to be taken down but slowly enough to be understood so that the pupils would know the kind of thing that would be appropriate; then writing it in "their own words"—words which approximate to what the teacher said but which cannot be written without the desirable effort. (*1957 Handbook*).

When practices of this kind occur, the subject knowledge may appear to be learnt, but at the cost of an utter divorce between language and experience. More often the "knowledge" will not be learnt and the "desirable effort" will be pitifully directed at following a linguistic model, as in this passage by a twelve-year-old who certainly did not find writing easy:

> There are five petals on a buttercup. It is a shape of a heart it is yellow and it is sticky. It has lines and shiney one side and dull. I have got 31 stamen. The stamen are long it has got spots and it begins to bubble. A cactus is like a pincushion and a cocnut. The little spot are like a carpel . . .

The diagnosis will probably be offered that this pupil "couldn't take it". Quite so.

If pupils are to take from a subject what it has to offer, all specialists must realize the roles that language plays. Traditionally, language has been viewed as a "vehicle" for knowledge, a conception encouraged by the appearance in notebooks and examination papers of words that echoed those printed in the textbook. (In the process, knowledge has been reified, see p. 11.) The significance of talk has been too often ignored, though it is increasingly used in the new developments of school maths, science, etc. A personal response has been felt to be rather irrelevant: why trouble about "what is going on inside pupils when they are given a frog to dissect or stop to admire the bright blue inside a test-tube or are moved by a moment of history"?

As teachers of English we need to present a different view of language, showing how certain varieties embody different strategies in handling experience, and how *all* varieties grow from a relatively undifferentiated matrix. In general we have to reinforce those subject specialists who are increasingly realizing that, for instance, scientists are not made by teaching pupils the passive voice and the avoidance of the second person, but by inculcating awarenesses and attitudes (towards certain kinds of data) that will draw on the necessary linguistic forms. Further research is badly needed into the stages by which, principally in talk and interaction, a pupil best learns to adapt to specialist purposes the language he already uses. This requires a willingness on the part of subject specialists, in the sciences for instance, to allow for a *gradual* development of scientific purposes in language, rather than to impose a sudden switch. Then they will be less likely to meet writing that fumbles after the teacher's words and formulation, as in the last example, and more likely to find something that speaks of a personal effort to look at an object with the curiosity and detachment that may grow into a scientific attitude:

First we got a glass dish and a microscope. Then we got a buttercup and we took the petals off.

The petals came off very easy. There were five petals. on the head. And the petals were in the shape of a heart.

Its yellow and its shiney and it has lines on it. The shiney part is the inside of the petal when it is closed ... Then we got the head of the buttercup stamens.

And then we pulled off all the stamens and counted them and I had 52. Then we put one under a microscope and it was long and spotty it is also thick and covered at the end. There are two things on it, they are called pollen box and fillament ...

When an uncertain writer like this pupil is focusing on the experience and not on the teachers' words, he can achieve surprising control.

*　　　*　　　*

Teachers of English have an important, integrating role to play it is true. Their primary concern is with the levels of experience and the matrix of language from which all specialist concerns develop. Starting from the family, friends and neighbourhood, its work and play, what preoccupations, interests and problems (they ask) arise as a child and teenager pushes back the frontiers of experience and has to bring new territories into living relationship with the old?

If in English a child keeps alive to new possibilities in the familiar centres of experience, there is some chance of other teachers encouraging successful exploration in untracked areas of science, history, etc. If the encounter with new territory is a lively one (not a conducted tour dictated by the bus driver), there will be repercussions in the older, central areas. Each territory in turn becomes old and familiar: it relates and connects in more and more complex ways with the primary centres of life. So these three processes in language combine together to help or hinder individual growth. These are the concerns of English in its widest sense.

Chapter 4

A question of knowledge

"Knowing how the writer has gained his effects" is not the same thing as "being able to experience those effects as fully as possible"; and I suspect that there are all the world over too many teachers who are ready to concentrate on teaching about . . .

(Whitehead, Dartmouth)

One day a fussy pedagogue hired Nasrudin to ferry him across a very wide river. As soon as they were afloat the scholar asked if it was going to be rough.

"Don't ask me nothing about it," said Nasrudin.

"Have you ever studied grammar?"

"No," said the Mulla.

"In that case half your life has been wasted."

The Mulla said nothing. Soon a terrible storm blew up.

The Mulla's crazy cockleshell was filling with water. He leaned over to his companion. "Have you ever learnt to swim?"

"No," said the pedant.

"In that case, schoolmaster, all your life is lost for we are sinking."

('*The Exploits of the Incomparable Mulla Nasrudin*'
Shah, London, 1966)

Linguistic study seeks to make conscious and general that which is known in a way unconscious and particular. Clearly some such self-awareness is valuable for adults. But how far need it be systematized?

(Barnes, *N.A.T.E. Bulletin*)

The essential (in language study at college) is to start from a body of questions rather than a body of knowledge. Then, whatever the teacher has learnt can be used as appropriate; the other way the teacher is left with a fearful lack of confidence as a result of never having got beyond the threshold of a formal discipline.

(Strang, Dartmouth)

WITH regard to "knowledge" the two delegations passed each other in mid-Atlantic, as Nelson Francis remarked. Looked at from outside, the U.K. is the home of an educational tradition that throws the weight on examination syllabuses, rigorous and early specialism, and academic knowledge; the U.S., on the other hand, might be thought to stand for pragmatic learning, general education, and progressive schools. However, as we learnt, traditions change.

In the U.K. a breakaway from the constrictions of the tradition has recently given new emphasis to *experience* and to the *operational* use of language to handle, order and come to terms with it. After the initial shock of hearing this from British lips, there was some U.S. sympathy with this view. Increasingly in the U.S., there have been danger signs of examinations shaping courses of study—college board examinations, "standardized" exams given regularly throughout school, advanced placement examinations for the able, the threat of a new national assessment. On the other hand, the prevailing American concern seems to be with the danger at the other extreme of a chaotic approach to operational English associated with a "child-centred" curriculum in which the major concern was social adjustment and not a child's growth in intellectual, imaginative and linguistic power. Hence the recent attempts—still at the experimental stage—to try to affect operation through *knowledge*, and the building up of *programs* of learning—on the assumption that to promote growth, experience must come in some sort of order.

A reaction from tradition often brings its own kind of simplification. However, it is not the intention of this chapter to show that the answer lies in a sort of mid-Atlantic compromise. The usefulness of the debate on this issue was to provoke members to reconsider the terms and the principles from which they had started. Of these "knowledge" was the most important and elusive.

Traditionally, all academic subjects are considered to have a body of knowledge, a content. The debate opened with the provocative statement that English has *no* content. A body of information had been "thought up" in response to the example of the sciences and the demands of examiners. Its effect was to distort and fragment the teaching of English. "If the readers and writers of this paper take stock of what knowledge and proficiency they attained at school and university and considered how much of their attainment has remained actively with them, what would be the result? Very little, one suspects. It would probably be a humbling exercise for us as teachers" (Thompson).

In such a context the word "content" probably implies explicit knowledge in systematic order, pre-planned by the teacher so that the student can as it were take it away with him (all packaged) when he leaves school. In British contexts such "knowledge" probably collocates with "instruction"—used here in a narrower sense than an American would expect? There was fairly wide agreement that in English we are not concerned with a content quite like that. The same may be true for many subjects, in their more recent interpretation. But "knowledge" may be interpreted as something less as well as more explicit, and may arise from pupils learning as well as teachers instructing. A polarized notion of "knowledge" was a hindrance to discussion; one needed to consider "working knowledge" and "conscious proficiency", relating both of them to *awareness*.

Some ways of "knowing" are intensely personal; where they are, the process of learning may be painfully slow. Holbrook has described how it took a girl over a year of brooding and writing to face and articulate what the experience of her mother's death meant to her. This kind of knowledge is bound up with the entire affective aspect of our lives.

The teacher can do little more than make available a variety of situations in which, if the pupil chooses, the knowledge may gradually become explicit and controllable.

At other times, for example when pupils are prone to criticize a new classmate's dialect, we can encourage explicit knowledge much more directly, clarifying by question, discussion and study the idea of "accent" and "dialect". But we have to admit that modifying social attitudes as deeply ingrained as these involves more than a new level of *conceptual* awareness. Before such knowledge can be said to be "useful" a pupil may have to commit himself to a process just as complex as the healing of his emotional wounds. Think of the case of the fourteen-year-old whose class had been analysing in groups the daily newspapers, using a set of criteria that they themselves had drawn up in discussion: "You know," she said, "that paper we get at home is rubbish, and we've proved it—but I feel sure I'll go on reading it."

One Seminar group looked further at knowledge *in use* in moment by moment experience. As we make choices, decisions and judgements we draw on past experience, which is available to us in the form of knowledge as well as other forms. When we talk of a body of knowledge or a set of ideas, we imply that some parts of our past experience have been organized cognitively. If a choice or decision is difficult to make and requires thinking over, we use these organized ideas as a frame of reference in discussing the issue. They partly determine the way we look at the issue; in fact as we approach an act of choice our past experience builds up certain expectations about the form the choice will take.

Of course, in ordinary living no choice, decision or judgement is made without consideration of what we *feel* as well as what we *know*. But it seems that feelings are not organized in the same way as knowledge, and that as cognitive frames of reference are built up they have to be divorced and isolated from the influence of our desires and feelings about the world. A subject or discipline—history or geography, for example—can be regarded as a cognitive frame of reference of this kind.

However, in our day-to-day relations with other people and the choices and decisions that are continually involved, it is probably not the cognitive frame of reference but the structure of feelings that matters most. If we do appeal to knowledge it may well be to "common sense", a primitive form of organization that perhaps incorporates both cognitive and affective elements at low levels of generality. As pupils talk, write and read in English lessons they are structuring experience, sometimes in terms of common sense, sometimes as patterns of feeling, or again as more comprehensive frames of reference. Consequently, bodies of knowledge—about life, about books, about words—are among the products of their work. It is possible to regard these bodies of knowledge as the "content" of the subject English, though not everyone would be happy with this view.

If we are asked to define a curriculum for English there seems to be a choice between, on the one hand, indicating the broad areas of experience with which we are concerned—where we want to see language used in bringing things to order—and, on the other, indicating the frames of reference that we expect to emerge. When we choose the first, we are inevitably either general and vague, talking about "personal worlds" and "relationships with people day by day", etc., or concrete and patchy, talking in terms of family and neighbourhood, the world of work and leisure, etc. When we choose the second, we can be rather precise for some cognitive frames of reference, but at the expense of feeling and common sense, the kinds of knowledge that fit less well into the traditional form of curriculum guides. This is the problem already encountered on p. 33 in discussing the true "lessons" of English, and it is the stumbling-block whenever we discuss what is meant by "knowledge" of literature.

Each method of definition has limitations, then, and either way we may miss the heart of the matter. Conversely, providing we are alert to their limitations, both may be useful. On this view, then, a switch from "areas of experience" to "bodies of knowledge" is a change of perspective on a process that actually incorporates both. By convention, a syllabus or curriculum guide tends to be phrased in terms of the bodies of knowledge that are hoped for. Can we agree that in the past (and at present) this has misled many teachers into pressing for the body of knowledge at the expense of the rest of the process? This misconception has had very far-reaching consequences. Take, for instance, the Latinate grammar that most of us British teachers had inculcated in us at school: only too often the syllabus became the lesson, and each week gerunds or gender or whatever were handed to us as neat end products. That part of the process where a pupil draws on (or refers back to) experience was short-circuited; thus it was not often discovered that gender was irrelevant to English anyway. By concentrating on the body of knowledge the teacher can *assume* the relevance of what he is handing over—or, more honestly, the question of relevance never enters his head. Instead a tradition is accepted.

Here is the danger that many of us (on both sides of the Atlantic) foresee in the proposals to introduce the teaching of new and superior English grammars to the schools. Despite different intentions on the part of those producing materials, teachers who have already invested a good deal in the traditional grammar may simply switch to a new body of knowledge, without giving a thought to the process whereby such knowledge could ever come to be *in use*. The process of arriving at forms of knowledge that affect judgements, choices, and decisions would once again have been short-circuited. And ironically this might well be done under the label of a new "humanistic" study of language.

To be aware of the danger is not to damn all linguistic discussion in school. Rather we need to seek a clearer definition of the circumstances in which conceptualizing of linguistic awareness is likely to arise in class. There is no certainty at present which areas of experience, at what times in a child's development, will tend to raise in pupils the first fumbling demands for a cognitive frame of reference that involves linguistics. Becoming aware of one's own dialect (or another pupil's), learning the graphemic systems, and second language learning, are just three possibilities. As a consequence of the first uncertainty there is a second and equal one as to which linguistic theory will prove the most appropriate. It was proposed at the Seminar that a suitable theory must enable a teacher "to move towards assessing the success of an utterance on a particular occasion. It must include an elaborate treatment of the nature of specialized varieties of a language. It must come to grips with the central concepts of style, correctness and acceptability. For some time now linguists have tended to take too narrow a view of their subject matter . . . [thus] at the present time, 'correct English' and 'good style' are terms from different, if not incompatible, areas of the subject; from the pragmatic point of view they are different stages of the same process, that of creating effective utterances" (Sinclair). If this view is correct the first call is for further developments in linguistics.

At present we are rather ignorant about three things: first, the ways in which children and young people learn language; second, the conditions and the stages in which they become aware of language they have learnt to use; and third, the effects of such awareness or knowledge on their further learning and operating of language. For the first, we need work by the linguists (especially those with a foot in psychology and sociology); for the second we need observations by teachers concerned to draw out and develop pupils' awarenesses, rather than impose their own; for the third, we need inter-disciplinary studies and experiments. But the insights of the first should inform the second, the second the third, and so on.

Turning from the problems for linguists and for research to those of the classroom, the Seminar had two major recommendations to make. Past research has tended to show that teaching Latinate grammar does not help pupils to use language effectively; however, with new grammars, this may no longer be the case and pending the results of carefully designed experiments (and some but not all of those at present under way deserve the title), we must leave the issue open. Thus "it may be possible to provide sets of ordered language experiences which will work toward the development of the student's flexibility and agility and general command as a user of his native tongue" (Marckwardt). But there exists a curiosity about language much wider than that of the grammatical level, and here teachers of literary and linguistic background share an interest. On this broader front, observant teachers, informed with the spirit of recent linguistic work, may well find many unsuspected places where conceptualizing about language develops unnoticed at present. It was a common concern of the Seminar that pupils should be freed from *disabling conceptions* of "correctness" and "dialect", to mention two examples. This negative criterion is of major importance while (by modern linguistic standards) so much of the folk-linguistics that pupils meet inside school as well as outside is "corrupt and sometimes offensive" (Strang). But a further, positive criterion was also proposed. "Teaching which aims at leading students outward from their sense of language as an artifact, a given, to a sense of themselves as organizers of experience in the act of speaking and writing (or reading) . . . is an absolutely invaluable part of the life of the English classroom." This is a matter for linguistic as well as literary insights, for perceptions, that is, depending on a linguistic frame of reference however slight. Although these two criteria still leave unsettled—as the Seminar did—what work will arise, they offer principles of selection to guide teachers in undertaking such work.

The second recommendation proposes not a kind of knowledge but the way it should arise. There is still the danger that a teacher will stuff concepts into children before they are ready, and the converse danger that he will never allow or encourage enabling conceptions to develop. There is the traditional belief that "we need to teach in the third form what will be of some benefit in the fourth" —though not directly in the third. All these have been sure ways of stifling the interests and curiosity of children in language. So "no pupil should ever be pushed to the point of conceptualization until he is so steeped in the level of operation that he pushes himself to that level. Ideally, no pupil should ever be given an assignment which does not, at that time in the class, yield him enough fruit in his own terms, so that he can feel it was worth doing. We should never, in other words, impose the future upon the pupil unless we can find some way to translate it into the present" (Booth).

When we teachers tell ourselves (in syllabuses and curricular guides) that pupils *should* be familiar with this or that literature, *should* have a working knowledge of this or that rhetorical form, *should* be aware of varieties of English, differences in standard, etc.— in all these cases we are in effect giving ourselves a reminder of what to be looking for in pupils' discoveries. These are the things the teacher is bearing in mind, waiting for the pupils to reach towards, looking for an opportunity to develop. So there are two levels: at the first, the structure the teacher bears in mind; at the other, his observation of the individual's development and his sense that at some point in that development, this is the appropriate moment—to judge by the pupil's signals—for the creation of a particular frame of reference to be meaningful. Thus, a discussion of the attitudes, feelings and ideas implied by a word, according to its context, may arise in reading a poem aloud, or in looking at an advertisement, or when a class that has just been reading, say, Hemingway suddenly turns to Dylan Thomas; indeed there are so many occasions for awareness of this kind to come to the surface through a hesitation, a question, or an argument, that it seems quite unnecessary for teachers suddenly to impose a set course on elementary semantics.

Linguistic discussions, then, arise from the pupils' own questions and observations on the language they use and naturally meet (real language in operation, not textbook fabrications that have no other purpose—no reference to experience that involves the class).

And here we come to a final crux. In the course of discussion that arises from pupils' questions and comments on language, we teachers (for our own sakes) need to be able to relate what arises to a broader frame of reference that we ourselves have derived from linguistic theory, and to some extent this frame needs to be general and systematic. But how far do we expect pupils to engage in system building? To some extent our answer depends on the level of conceptualization at which a particular system develops. There is a sense in which all children in so far as they learn to read and write become *aware* of the systems of graphemics, for instance. Here, conceptualization is primitive and intimately related to the operational use of language. But gradually alongside such discussions we believe there will be others—equally spontaneous—where conceptualizing is less directly related to operation and more abstract. These scattered and discrete discussions will finally *create* the study of language, a study which "would stand among other studies of a socio-scientific nature as an option in the higher grades of High School or in the Sixth Form. Its purpose would be to free a student from disabling misconceptions about language by giving him some of the tools of linguistic thought, rather than take him through an exhaustive study of grammar". It would *study problems*, as Acton advised, for from such studies a body of knowledge is gradually *drawn in*, for the sake of its relevance in providing a frame of reference within which the issues can be effectively discussed.

About knowledge as part of English, then, we can speak at present in principle only, not in particular. However, there are two instances that were discussed in detail at the Seminar. The first comes from the literary, not the linguistic field. How appropriate, we asked ourselves, was the frame of reference offered by such school texts as the histories of American Literature? We were in broad agreement that such knowledge should be rejected. The erection of a historical or geographical frame of reference for literature has, in our view, seriously limited the way school teachers and pupils have looked at literary texts, focusing attention on things external to experience of the text itself. In the upper classes at school and possibly (probably?) in the early years at college, very few students are prepared for a systematic framework of this kind—it does not meet their needs in reading literature.

The second instance was, in fact, so detailed that it can only be referred to here. What, we were asking, is the relevance of the linguist's body of knowledge—frame of reference—to the literary man's perceptions? Our question was answered empirically in a prepared discussion of Graves' poem "Legs" by John Sinclair and Wallace Robson. In the course of the discussion it became clear that often the perceptions which we define in literary criticism have been

G

organized at an unconscious level by perceptions that the linguist is well aware of and very well able to talk about. There was in fact a kind of substratum in the way Robson had worked on the poem that was explored and made fully articulate by Sinclair. The exposition of the order and system in the poem in terms of its linguistic structure offered an important verification of literary intuitions. Better still, as Robson said, "Sometimes we differ, and that's interesting I think, and one has to see whether one has found something that perhaps he hasn't, or perhaps he's seen something that I haven't."

Broadly speaking, it seems that linguistics can potentially make available to the literary man many of the non-verbalized or unconscious processes in his response to a text. On these his criticism is based. Thus a kind of verification procedure for his intuitions is available—though, like the computer, the linguist is exhaustive rather than selective in assembling preliminary information, so that his method will probably be used more sparingly than the literary critic's.

To sum up: the testing point for a model of English based on *experience* and language *in operation* will be its account of knowledge and of programmes (for the latter see the next chapter). We can usefully look on "bodies of knowledge" as frames of reference for *actions*—for judgements, choices and decisions. In these terms, subject specialists in, say, history or geography are concerned among other things with developing cognitive frames of reference which will help account for certain areas of experience. But in ordinary living we judge, choose and make decisions in terms of feelings, desires and attitudes which have their own forms of organization. The structuring of experience that we aim for in English certainly involves the affective as well as the cognitive. This raises a difficult choice when we try to define the English syllabus or curriculum, whether in terms of experience to be organized or in terms of frames of reference to be developed.

Because for convenience the syllabus or curriculum is often phrased in terms of a body of knowledge, rather than the activities which it helps to guide and steer, there has been and still is a predilection among specialist teachers for "feeding in" the frame of reference still in its abstract form. This in effect first by-passes the process whereby pupils learn for themselves to build and extend their frame of reference and, second, generally precludes the use of the inculcated body of knowledge as a basis for future action. (Often this error goes unnoticed because the examinations test for body of knowledge, not for its availability in action.)

When we taught traditional grammar we could not, as research showed, claim to affect language in operation. In fact grammar teachers, both past and present, have been among those most guilty of imposing a body of knowledge which never became a guide to action or a point of reference. It may be, however, that newer grammars will affect language in operation; that remains to be demonstrated.

On the other hand, language is an area where many misconceptions have grown up in school, just at the time when modern linguistics has been developing a frame of reference that enables us to comprehend them. Thus, teachers need to be familiar enough with modern linguistics to be able to draw from the subject a framework in which to understand the problems of language in class.

But it would be folly for teachers of English to impose linguistic bodies of knowledge on pupils. If a pupil has sensed that there is a problem or an issue, and is perhaps struggling to find terms in which it can be discussed, he will see the point of having a frame of reference. He must learn to solve his own problems, guided by the teacher whose awareness and broader frame of reference gives him a better perspective—and a better chance of seeing the pupils' difficulties and encouraging them to emerge.

We must remind ourselves therefore that the "body of knowledge" in a syllabus or curriculum guide represents our hopes of what pupils will discover and build as discussion arises from day to day, not a package to be handed over. It is the package idea that prompts for example such school studies as History of American Literature, studies that deflect the pupil from the living experience that literature could offer.

While we cannot offer detailed guidance, we do propose two broad criteria whereby teachers can judge when and in what direction to develop discussion of language in class: the first concerns disabling misconceptions, the second, more generally, points to the way that linguistic as well as literary disciplines offer us a vision of ourselves as organizers of experience in the act of speaking, reading and writing.

Chapter 5

Continuity—in what sense?

The Americans, without the dubious benefits of continuity provided by the British system of examinations, often feel they have precious little continuity at all.

(Working party, Dartmouth)

The search for "structure" as a guiding principle leads to a retrogressive emphasis on "knowledge" (knowledge about the language, or about literature).

(Whitehead, Dartmouth)

The Commission's proposed answer to the question "What literature should the English teacher know and teach?" is not a definition, not a master list. . . . What the Commission seeks is a clearer understanding of the consensus that it believes already exists, though it is nowhere fully realized . . . (and) a consensus means an agreement arrived at through consultation and common consent.

(Commission on English, 1965)

You wanted us to come up with something less specific than a curriculum and more ordered than chaos.

(Eastman, Dartmouth)

WHEN teachers demand programmes and systems of knowledge, we can read this as an expression of a deeply felt need for a sense of order and sequence in their day-to-day work. The activities described in Chapter 3 stress the need for improvisation, for observing and meeting pupils' interests as they emerge, for sounding out responses rather than presupposing them—for a flexible way of teaching English. But improvisation can become sloppy, makeshift and even

overwhelming unless it is sustained by a clear sense of broad underlying patterns. Looked at from this point of view, it was agreed that
every teacher is working with a structure. This is implied by his
decisions about what books to take in, for example, to read with a
fourteen-year-old class. "Behind those decisions is an implicit
concept of sequence. Perhaps I should not say concept; the whole
point here is that it is apt to be buried. We can all cite cases of
teachers operating on hidden premises. ... It is a question of un-
earthing them, looking at them, and seeing if we believe in them or
not" (Moffett). The underlying pattern we work to may be laid down
by examinations (as so often in the U.K.), or it may be largely
traditional (an acceptance of the way we ourselves were taught), or it
may derive from a theory—fully or partially developed—of English
teaching. Whatever the case, the present generation of teachers have
felt an increasing pressure on such patterns from two social forces.

The first results from geographical mobility: thus in the U.S.
today 20 per cent of all families are changing residence every year,
and a half of these move across state lines. Though this is probably
not equalled in G.B. at large, it will certainly be paralleled in some
urban growth areas. Part of this movement of course is a movement
of teachers. Thus the Newsom report (1963), commenting on the
English secondary modern schools—the schools attended by
the majority of pupils aged eleven to fifteen—stated that "of the
teachers who were on the staff when the pupils entered the schools
in 1958, only half the women were still there in 1961, and about two-
thirds of the men. Not only had many new teachers come, but there
had been a great many comings and goings in between."* Without a
fairly strong tradition of English teaching in the school, the district,
and finally in the country, the effort to adapt that is demanded of
pupils and teachers must be wasteful and even destructive. But social
forces are against steady, long-term tradition, and this is our second
point: "no longer can we depend upon so much of what [we felt]
used to be simply part of the culture ... a knowledge of the Bible,
for one thing, a knowledge of mythology, a knowledge of folklore"
(Marckwardt). Popular culture, depending so strongly on the media
for mass-communication, is subject to continual change and some
debilitation perhaps.

* *Half our Future*, H.M.S.O., 1963.

Under such pressures there is a tendency to panic, to define an external curriculum—a system into which teacher and pupil must fit—instead of helping teachers, in departments and larger groups, to define for themselves the order and sequence that underlies their best work. There was considerable agreement at the Seminar that such panic measures were to be avoided (with important implications, to be discussed later, for development work in curriculum centres). The major question then was to decide in what terms we might expect the underlying systems to be expressed.

Our starting point was a careful evaluation by Frank Whitehead of the structuring principles at present under consideration. Whitehead's conclusions, which can only be summarized here, were as follows: efforts to derive a sequential curriculum from "the basic principles of structure in literature" or from "basic recurring themes" have been essentially arbitrary, deflective, and restrictive. Further, while it was true that the growing child develops in the complexity of his sentence structure, in the size of his vocabulary, and in the control of paragraph organization, research offers no basis for a sequential programme 5–18 (or K–12) based simply on these linguistic levels. "To the external observer, then, the attempt to derive a rational sequence for the teaching of English from the internal structure of the subject as studied at its highest level seems open to three major objections. In the first place, there is no body of agreement as to the nature of this structure, nor does any such agreement seem attainable; it is not even clear whether it should be looked for within the discipline of literary criticism or that of linguistics. Secondly, the search for this kind of 'structure' as a guiding principle leads to a retrogressive emphasis on 'knowledge' (knowledge *about* the language, or *about* literature) as opposed to 'ability to use'. And, thirdly, the desire for a step-by step articulation leads* (as is made explicit in Hook, 1962) to a demand that the English teacher's field of activity be restricted to that which can be made incremental."

Not everyone in the Seminar agreed with this conclusion, but a detailed reply did not emerge. Perhaps one will still be made. Meanwhile it seems fair to say that hopes for a definition in terms of "the great and simple structuring ideas" are fed by the illusion that all subjects are akin to Mathematics. Not much consideration is

* J. N. Hook, *English Journal*, N.C.T.E., 1962.

needed to show that Mathematics and English are worlds apart, or to put it another way, the world shaped through natural language is much less simple and homogeneous than that expressed through the mathematical. As we have seen, English is the meeting point of experience, language and society. It implies "a developmental pattern whose origin and momentum come from outside the school situation, and which is intimately bound up with the individual's whole intellectual, emotional, social and spiritual growth" (Whitehead). Such a pattern will be complex and will draw on several disciplines (including psychology and sociology) for a balanced description.

Thus it seems an elementary mistake to demand a list of skills, proficiencies and knowledge as the basis for an English curriculum. Demands of this kind produce two wrong kinds of answer: answers so detailed that we determine, let's say, the books every child should read by a particular stage; or answers so general that the skills, etc., described are not amenable to being put in order one after the other. What is needed, if we are to clarify our sense of continuity, is not a single level of abstraction but a hierarchy of levels.

To start at a fairly concrete level: a teacher asked to suggest a new book to a ten-year-old may think of something similar to the last one (*The Hobbit* after a C. S. Lewis story), or something quite different (like *Wind in the Willows*). Each individual's line of education is continuous and discontinuous in this sense. A completely predetermined or one-track list of assignments in reading leaves no room for individual growth or initiative. But neither is throwing the library at the student a real opportunity for free choice. Stage by stage a teacher sets up a framework of choice within which she helps a pupil to find his own purposes. Books offer the simplest framework of course. We set up a classroom library, dip into books with pupils, encourage them to choose a book to read, take up the experience of favourite books in drama and talk . . .: so long as the framework of choice and the stimulus to read are rich enough, and the chances for reading are there, the process is self-sustaining. (*A priori* theories are more likely to restrict what we make available—whether to fairy-tale or blood and thunder—than empirical experiment and observation of what pleases individuals.) But books are conveniently self-contained experiences: the broader experience on which we draw—of people and situations, of oneself and one's environment—is more amorphous. Again, however, our best guides are the things pupils come up and talk about, hanging on after school perhaps—their individual and group interests (however expressed) rather than an external "guide" or textbook (which necessarily cannot know their particular circumstances). On a day-by-day level, that is, continuity depends on a flow of talk between pupils and teacher, a questing exploratory atmosphere, a sensitive ear to emerging feelings and ideas and a rich sense of their thematic possibilities and connections. At this level, a teacher's art lies in taking a pupil where he is interested and in some sense sharing with him the search for new possibilities. Her knowledge is an awareness of human experience as the child or youngster sees it, and of the insights into it that may be possible through talk, reading, drama and writing. The point about the teacher's knowledge is that, like the pupil's, it is not static and once for all, but alive and growing through her entering into the experience of others (and her inner self), in reality and in imagination.

Still at a concrete level, but generalizing from it: a teacher choosing books to set aside as possibles for reading and discussing with a fourteen-year-old class will consider some that appeal (he imagines or knows from experience) to a particular level of maturation in insight and interest. Most students, that is, seem to follow a roughly common process of maturation and psychological development, which in some sense is continuous and sequential. Teachers often work from their intuitive awareness of this continuity—or more properly perhaps their empirical awareness, as they sense new pre-occupations arising in the talk, writing and drama of dominant groups of the class. Sometimes a knowledge of the psychology of child development and the sociology of sub-cultures which affect this pattern will make a teacher alive to aspects he had not noticed, or directions he had been hazy and uncertain about. The difficulty is that not enough is known at this level. We are broadly aware that in terms of fictions, "children begin with the capacity to conceive characters in flat terms. They conceive the people they see around them in these terms, I think, except the very close people. The central group for them is the family group. Nature is personified; it has a face and movement of its own. They like this kind of literature. This is what they read and what they like to have read to them—folk literature in which the family is the central group, in which most characters are flat and melodramatic, in which nature has a mythic face (Olsen). At the beginning of the story there is the mother and the father or just the mother, and at the end of the story, if it is the Cinderella type, there is a marriage and somebody goes riding off and lives happily ever after. There aren't the other kinds of groups, the work group, the office group, or any of the groups by which we live." Maybe a lot of English teaching at this stage has to do with the interaction between living experience of human relationships and the fictions that are used to interpret them. There does seem to be a strong polarization of fantasy and reality, and we need to know a good deal more about this.

At the later stage of adolescence, "the stresses of the period may force pupils to erect barriers against the direct expression of emotion that may be found in literary works, most conspicuously in some kinds of poems", or may over-simplify emotional response into gush, hysteria, or sentimentality. Pupils may "seek the safety of conformity to mass attitudes, or participating in mass responses; may refuse to express response, not because of a total flight from response, but because of peer group pressures not to put it into so many words. They may assert an adult utilitarian calculus—What good is all this?—; or among better and older students, have recourse to literary criticism and explicit [permitted] responses representing perhaps an early capitulation to adult standards."*Again we need to know more. Is E. Z. Friedenberg right in claiming that, in adolescence especially, education is designed to "starve out, through silence and misrepresentation, the capacity to have genuine and strongly felt experience, and to replace it by the conventional symbols that serve as the common currency of daily life. . . . It is still the spontaneous, vivid and immediate that is most feared, and feared the more because so much desired by [adults]" ?† At such points the evidence from psychology meets with that from cultural studies: hence the relevance of Hoggart's study, *The Uses of Literacy*, to teachers in the older working class districts of England and the need for further extended analyses of the many worlds in which a pupil becomes involved "in the fictions he encounters in popular culture".

At a different level of abstraction, one aspect of maturation is linguistic. We begin to see that as a student learns to take on new

* *Response to Literature*, N.C.T.E., 1969.
† *Dignity of Youth*, Boston, 1960.

roles within his group and to act out some of the dominant roles in his society, he is learning to use new varieties of language (marked most obviously by vocabulary and "accent", but also by the predominant structures and other less obvious features—pause frequency and length, the amount and forms of redundance, for example). Such role learning probably has runs and sequences, though it is hardly likely to have one continuous line, and one would expect much recapitulation and development. At present we are becoming aware of unnecessary discontinuities between, on the one hand, spoken varieties of English among five- to seven-year-olds and, on the other, the first written forms they are asked to read (see p.16). Mapping the whole field of varieties of discourse as these emerge among pupils five to eighteen will be a complex job, though a start is already being made (under the Schools Council of England & Wales). In so far as it is successful, this mapping work may suggest not only simple runs but also a prerequisite set of stages in which the individual needs *experience* (role and situation) if we are to see emerging the varieties of *language* necessary to mature discussion in higher education, for example. Meanwhile (and in any case) we teachers need to keep the range of situations and roles wide, and persistently to look for possible extensions suggested by the class's work.

A final and very schematic approach was tentatively suggested by Jim Moffett. If we wanted to map the relevant patterns of growth we should need to look from more than one point of view at the field of language-operating-on-experience. Social and cultural variables raise the need for new varieties of language to meet new roles and situations. Psychological and behavioural variables, sometimes overlapping with social forces, modify the level of conceptualization and the affective or cognitive loading with which language is used. A map that brings these together is probably theoretically possible, and may well be desirable, not for minute by minute use in class of course, but as an integrating system that could help teachers of English make explicit (particularly to their colleagues) the sorts of general development they are working for with particular classes. It would map, and thus help us to see in a detailed, organized way, continuities on a year by year timescale or longer. If we think of language as a system of representation, then progression will lie in the quality of the representation and its fit with experience at different levels. If we think of language more dynamically as a method of organizing, then progression will lie in new forms of organizing experience and in additional refinement or complexity. Among the continuities noted during the Seminar were the following:

(*a*) Using language, a young child like Stephen (p. 24) moves from the immediate and present experience to what is coming next, to the past, and finally to potential rather than actual experience ("And if you do have a truck in there it won't work"). Working in this way children learn to move from the realm of events to the realm of logical possibilities. This seems to relate to Walter Loban's observation of a growth in the expression of tentativeness: "There were lots of newts in the pond t-day I daresay they like this kind of weather", says the ten-year-old on p. 5, and this speculation seems typical of a certain kind of maturity.

(*b*) When children first begin to tell stories, their language again becomes independent of the immediate present and the on-going activities, but in a different way. "A story is symbolically more powerful because more selective, more summary, more explicit in reference" (Moffett). Story gives children an opportunity to represent things in general, not just the particular here-and-now. How far this process of universalizing and generalizing takes us is suggested by Janice's piece written at the age of eight (p. 7).

(*c*) In developing these symbolic stories and representations children may begin by projecting out into very remote figures, like a dragon or even a kitten (p. 26), but, as they mature, there is a movement like that from myth to naturalistic fiction; by Ian's age they may have learnt in addition to use the world of here-and-now directly as the substance of their stories and themselves as the characters.

(*d*) As we grow we become more capable of setting down explicitly some of the things implicit in our language and gestures. This is the broad difference between "Oh, Ian," and "I was in trouble again" (p. 50), where the growth in explicitness in some sense modifies the understanding of people and oneself. There is an effort towards explicitness in a rather different vein in the description of dissecting a buttercup (p. 68). It may be that whenever we concentrate on fitting language more closely to experience there will be either a growth in explicitness or an extension in the range of implicit connections, or both. From this point of view children's narrative is an early means of embodying implicit connections that may later become explicit generalizations and theoretical statements.

(e) Young children start with a small, immediate and familiar audience, but gradually learn to meet and talk with unknown and "distant" people; in doing so they develop new varieties of language. In their monologue (especially after it has moved over into writing) they may later learn to build imaginatively an audience that is large and unknown, and to adapt their language accordingly.

(f) We move from language about people and things to language about language. In doing so we may gain a new control over the linguistic method of representing and organizing experience. Theoretically it seems that the ability to "operate on operations" ought to bring us new power, as it certainly does in the language of mathematics. Perhaps we ought to look critically and selectively at linguistics, then, to assess its dynamic possibilities rather than its static descriptions?

Clearly a model incorporating such diverse forms of progression would be extremely complex. Perhaps, as in the Seminar, the tendency would be to isolate two or three major parameters—for example, modes of discourse and ways of thinking. If so, we might note beforehand the danger of seeing such progressions as a simple, linear matter. Thus, we should remember that, just as man oscillates between the here-and-now and the dream at all stages in his life, so the literature of actuality will be read alongside the literature of fantasy: the one does *not* replace the other. Indeed it might be felt that from Piers Plowman to Kafka there is "a narrative that unites inner and outer, here-and-now and dream". Further, the traditional emphasis on cognitive growth (in ways of thinking) tends to focus attention away from the equally important stages in the accommodation to modes of feeling, judging and evaluating that characterizes the reading of literature (including personal writing). "We should also make it quite clear that at every stage our literary experience will have four simultaneous stages: what the pupil (a) writes, (b) speaks, (c) reads, and (d) has read to him, will offer different levels of affective and cognitive experience. For instance, a written story will at the youngest age be episodic for mechanical reasons, and, at the other extreme, a story read to the child may be able to communicate more advanced cognitive and affective experience, mediated as it is by the imagination, judgement, and sensibility of the adult." If such things are borne in mind there is less likelihood of this model encouraging, by feedback, an exclusive attention to linear progressions, neat as they are (Hardy).

To sum up: the natural need for a sense of order and sequence has to be recognized. Improvisation can thrive only within a framework that expresses, more or less articulately, an underlying pattern of development. We resist, however, the temptation to respond to the dynamics of social change by imposing a static and external curriculum on the schools. Nor will *a priori* systems modelled on subjects other than English really be of much help as a guide. Teachers locally and nationally need to discuss the best of their practice and in doing so to discover more of the underlying patterns that they intuitively follow. A day-to-day classroom method that nudges and encourages pupils as they take the initiative in organizing experience is compatible with a sense of long-term patterns. Unfortunately, we are short of detailed knowledge and analysis of psychological, social and linguistic patterns of growth. What knowledge we have can inform and develop our insight as teachers without determining our practice in detail. At present the danger is probably that simplified theory will inhibit good practice, though blindly empirical practice still flounders without theory. What we want is something less specific than a curriculum and more ordered than chaos. This means looking for continuity at more than one level of abstraction. In the course of such discussions mistakes of category seem an inevitable risk.

This should be added: if the question of continuity and programme means "What sort of product are you handing on to us?" and springs from a fear of impoverished standards in handling language, and of stunted curiosities about new experience and ideas, we answer that a new direction in English studies is indeed necessary and English departments operating the sort of activities we describe can show how this affects both language and openness to experience. In so far as the question comes from a desire for a standard package, we answer that it pays a college or a firm (like a school) to know the individual and work from there. In so far as the question is a demand for better information about performance, we sympathize and take a close look in the next chapter at the whole issue.

Chapter 6

An enquiry into examinations

Their power, their concern for the markable, is the chief reason for the continuance of that other version of "English" whose constituent parts are grammar, precis, spelling, comprehension, exercises, etc. It soon builds up into a self-sufficient subject with its own mechanical drive—its own techniques, tests, attendants, and its own minds, endorsed by and endorsing it.

(Jackson, *English versus Examinations*)

The drilling of a class in stereotyped questions based on past examination papers and luck . . . play a large part (in examination success at G.C.E.).

(*The Examining of English Language*, 1964)

The examination here has come to be dominated by what is termed psychometric elegance. . . .

(Purves, Dartmouth)

The curriculum in the secondary school inevitably shrinks to the boundaries of evaluation; if your evaluation is narrow and mechanical, this is what the curriculum will be.

(Loban, Dartmouth)

WE might begin by recalling the original sense of "examining": a close scrutiny, presumably of an on-going process. It is doubtful whether more than a tiny minority of the present examinations in English fulfil this definition, whether in school, college or university.

The range of English activities covered by present methods of examining in the U.K. and the U.S. is extremely narrow: talk and listening is often simply excluded, and drama almost always omitted. The situations constructed supposedly for sampling language in action narrow the range still further. Thus literature is examined but the texts are not available, unseen poems may not be read aloud, an eighteen-year-old in the U.S. is given 20 minutes for a composition and in the U.K. three major essays are demanded in three hours.

Procedures such as these will in themselves invalidate the work produced before it is scrutinized. But the form of scrutiny is pre-empted in most cases by the demand for a "reliable" mark on a scale that may range up to 600 points. The demand can be met in two ways. One reduces the examination to right/wrong questions, in which case everything in language that is partly-partly (not described by a two-valued logic) is neglected. Alternatively, the examiner may be asked to reach a complex series of judgements, in which case most of this information is discarded when his judgements are reduced to a single mark.

An assessment system that stopped there in its effects would be damaging enough. However, what happens beyond the examination room is often of more consequence. The tradition, especially in the U.K., is for preparation for the specialized uses of language demanded by the examinations to be fed back into the normal course; in the process, teachers and pupils often genuinely forget the natural uses of language to shape and order experience that really involves them. The examination itself begins to look quite normal, and English becomes a weird kind of game. Strategies of pleasing the examiner take precedence. We cannot be surprised that many students reject the restricted and unreal courses that result from this parody of the spiral curriculum (by exams, through exams, to exam success).

In both countries there are less rigid practices. In America particularly the problems have been raised and reconsidered over the years, sometimes at the instigation of the examining bodies themselves. In the U.K., where external examination pressures have had far deeper effects on the schools, the discussion provoked by the Certificate of Secondary Education and encouraged by the Schools Council has recently started off a radical reappraisal of examining. New attention is being given to the assessment of students by looking at work in progress, whether through U.S. course credit systems or through the methods of continuous assessment used in some of the English colleges of education and now being developed for C.S.E. and G.C.E. Even here, though, such is the prevailing feedback effect of external examinations that teachers often institute tests and "course exams" instead—that is, they trust the examination rather than course work. (Some U.S. firms in fact produce, presumably for this purpose, multiple choice tests on well-known literary texts.)

To sum up: the influence, actual and potential, of examinations and tests upon school curricula is increasing in both Britain and the United States. In the opinion of the Seminar a full and systematic review of examinations in English and grading practices of all kinds should be undertaken at once. What needs to be done in all three countries is to look critically at examinations, asking in the context of the aims and purposes of English such questions as the following:

(a) What are the purposes to which in general an examination or grading lends itself?

(b) Do the current examinations serve these purposes efficiently?

(c) Which of these purposes are educationally undesirable and which impede the teaching of English?

(d) What particular problems arise in connection with external examinations, and how should these be dealt with?

(e) Could alternative measures of attainment or perhaps an entirely different approach to the problem be devised and would it serve the purposes with less harm to good educational practice?

(f) Does a broadly imposed system of examinations and grading (national, regional, or state) lessen the sense of independence and responsibility with which teachers approach problems of assessing their own pupils' progress and diagnosing their difficulties?

Chapter 7

Implications for the school

With good classification (or grading) the city teacher can teach from 40 to 60 pupils well. In the ungraded school not even 16 to 30 pupils can be well taught.

(U.S. Commissioner of Education, 1894)

Each child in his own way is asking to be accepted, liked, taught and encouraged to become something more than he is today.

(Wilt, Dartmouth)

In order to achieve anything with these (disadvantaged) children the teacher has surely to completely reconsider his subject—and not only his subject, but even his conception of his function as an adult who has a professional duty to these children. What is he doing in that classroom? What can he possibly give those children? What can they possibly need from him? . . . Contact with these children often exposes the inadequacy of his own education.

(Holbrook, Dartmouth)

Not One Road or Many, but One Road and Many.

(Summerfield, Dartmouth)

EXAMINATIONS are only one way in which a school organization presupposes and exerts pressure towards a particular philosophy of education. Thus, we cannot expect change in the central activities of English, or Maths or Science, without implying changes in organization. As Holbrook remarked, "a school which inhibits spontaneity at large will be restricting the development of literacy" in its wider

95

H

sense—"the capacity to use words to deal with inner and outer experience".

To understand parts of the present organization we need to think historically. Each philosophy of education entails its own kind of educational structure. Thus the philosophy of skills implied:

- a schoolmaster on a dais, giving out class assignments, "correcting" the class work, organizing recurrent competitions in skill (tests);

- a class graded for its skill (the methods vary), disciplined to carry out the exact task set by the "Master", and to copy out again what they failed in;

- a classroom in which the main English equipment ended with the rows of desks, the "exercise" books, and the textbooks from which further exercises were drawn;

- a class period (lesson) of 30 minutes or so, adequate for taking on a new skill, with time for it to be explained, practice allotted, and results assessed.

There is a coherent approach behind this, not unfitted for the tasks then envisaged (instruction in routine elements of the three Rs), with very formally trained teachers. But the new approaches to English such as we suggest, and the analogous approaches now being developed in other subjects, are the results of a different philosophy and imply a totally different structure, parts of which are still to be explored.

Here perhaps is the greatest need to think through implications, tentatively but none the less rigorously. Both the skills and the heritage approach emphasized the teacher as authority, the class as recipients of instruction. Working on a developmental approach with activities such as we propose, a teacher has a complex relationship with pupils. Pupils learn to take on their own tasks within a framework of choice that the teacher introduces and helps them develop. Sometimes groups form themselves, sometimes a pupil works alone. Teachers spend more time planning initial experiences that suggest a branching programme of group or individual work: the class are called together at times when this seems appropriate— because they all need to share something. Oral, dramatic and written presentations by groups or by the whole class serve as focal points in long-term pieces of work: the class assesses what has been achieved (thinking it over and discussing what more might be tried). Simple marking or grading becomes irrelevant. What counts is recognition of one's part in a group achievement, or one's individual contribution to a class presentation (maybe in wall displays or on tape). In the class dialogue individuals realize when they have said something of value to the others: taken together these contributions amount to a collaborative learning of language and of what it makes of experience. Competition for marks or places becomes irrelevant: groups may compete occasionally but in general their work is complementary rather than simply parallel, and the effort is collaborative.

So changes in the central activities of the English classroom imply changes in the relations of teacher to pupil, of one pupil to another, and of group work to class work. These in turn suggest changes at three levels: in the classroom itself, in the English department, and in the school as a whole.

The English room

When we enter many of the best classrooms today we may well not see the desks laid out in their formal rows: they may be stacked well to the back while the class use the space for drama, or they may be grouped for display building or small discussions, or just for quiet reading. It is not enough to be able to face the blackboard: the class or group may be gathered round a thematic display of photographs or a tape recorder, may be discussing a filmstrip or watching a television screen. At some times of the day groups of pupils will be scattered round the room engaged in all these different activities: it has become an "open room" or "workshop". Spaces are planned to provide for a class library and quiet reading corner; a table for sacred objects like fossils, models and flowers; the visually attractive display of recent work, of charts and news sheets—with a glossary perhaps of local dialect; and if the school is lucky, something as useful as a sound-proofed tape recorder booth. In such classrooms the sterilized austerity of the old tiled walls is replaced by an attractive and enlivening environment; the room is as much the pupils' room as the teacher's. A lot more English classrooms should be equipped for this kind of use.

A "workshop" method, with individuals working with each other in groups of changing pattern, properly begins quite early on in primary or elementary school. It ought to develop fairly smoothly, though with new situations, into the secondary school. At present this is not happening. For example, many primary schools make an excellent start but then with specialist or departmental teaching the friendship and work groups are often abandoned, self-imposed tasks become a rarity, the rhythm of the day's work is broken up, and pupils seem to be regarded as a different breed of animal. Only rather late in the day does one discover interesting examples of the workshop approach, probably in the Sixth Form (with sixteen to eighteen year-olds), where pupils again become "responsible". Even the best English specialists in secondary schools tend to be cut off by training and practice from what the primary schools have pioneered, and to lose by such a discontinuity.

Do normal school conditions generally help the specialist or departmental teacher?—the 35 to 55 minute units for which the teacher normally sees the class, the relative isolation in which he works, the use of examination "success" as a long-term aim (perhaps to cover up or compensate for very short-term achievements in normal lessons?). How often do we still assume that the teacher is the main agent or even the only means by which the pupil is going to learn, and how can we reconcile this assumption with a growing need (internal and external) for independent action by young people? And what do we teachers (especially the subject teachers) know of a new pupil at the beginning of the school year? He brings with him his own cultural acquisitions, in part the result of his interaction with teachers of previous years, but also of his total achievement in the school: is it not rather depressing that quite often the only evidence of this that the teacher has is a mark or grade on a school report?

The department as a team

If we are to change the approach to English these and other conditions have to be questioned. But for an individual teacher to do so alone can easily be self-defeating. He or she needs the sharing of experience, the mutual encouragement and confirmation that a good department or larger group can offer. In the past the form of the English syllabus or curriculum guide has rarely had the effect of educating the teacher as he worked; actually it shielded him from the uncertainties and anxieties of change. Clearly the changes we envisage in English teaching will themselves bring uncertainty, and the kind of English we describe is itself a form of continuing education—a steady exposure to new experience in life. To sustain the tension of improvisation and the "untidiness" of a workshop classroom, teachers of English will need the security and springboard of ongoing discussions in the department and of their own "teachers' workshop" at a local centre. More positively, they will need to find means of sharing and joining in the best practice, making their own contribution as they do. So it may not be the best idea for the English specialist to retire into his classroom castle for all lessons. By decreeing this in the past, schools have shut off all the best teachers from their colleagues. No one sees them at work: their real value to other teachers is lost.

We foresee, therefore, times during the week for a team of English teachers, pooling interests and resources, to work together with a group of classes. There are many different ways in which such team teaching can be approached and, despite the many experiments already afoot, it may be some time before we know which forms are most appropriate to the central activities of English. Perhaps the change to a workshop classroom has to come first, so that pupils are already adapted to independence and group work; but then, again, many a teacher will take heart from the responsibility that pupils can show under team teaching and will feed this back into his own classroom.

The beginnings may be quite simple. For example, two or three classes come together to watch a film, to listen to some readings or a broadcast, or to go on a visit. Afterwards, in small groups of, say, 6–10 they will discuss things that arise, and as the teachers circulate (stimulating, nudging and correcting emphases in the discussions), propose follow-up activities. So, with help from the teachers according to the pupils' experience of independent work, a set of relevant assignments will be drawn up. These will be duplicated and circulated for pupils to think over in their own time: then, with discussion and guidance available from the team of teachers, choices will be made and work on the assignments begun, sometimes in pairs or individually, sometimes in larger groups. In the course of their work pupils or teachers may move freely between two or three workshop class-rooms, fitted up with the library and equipment (tapes, filmstrip, stimulating displays, teaching machines, etc.) needed for the job.

This is just one type of approach. In the course of it the most academic pupils may mix and work with the most down-to-earth: it is not hard to envisage times when the one will need the other, as exhibitions, tapes, plays or perhaps films are prepared. Groups of "mixed ability" in terms of the school subject may be rather similar, in terms of carrying out a co-operative enterprise. Teachers will initially concentrate on helping the group or individual to work independently, and on seeing that the assignments build up to a corporate achievement. Thus at certain phases all groups will be brought together to share in the enjoyment and the experience of the end products they have created.

At present, team teaching is in an experimental phase; some years may be needed before its possibilities have been imaginatively explored. Inevitably there will be problems to face and solve: how to balance, for example, work in a "home base" (with a class tutor) against the work with a team; how to ensure that the assignments do not lead back again to a fragmentation of English; how to keep the kind of communication that is achieved by a group of only 20 or 30 who know each other and their teacher well. No doubt there will be failures. Teams will need time— and some will not get it—not only for preparatory discussions but for careful evaluations. Nevertheless, if more teachers and pupils are to benefit from an open room or workshop approach, an overspill into team teaching is natural and right—and may well prove the best means of helping the newcomer and the "average teacher" gain experience and confidence in such new ways of learning. After all, there is abundant evidence that *pupils* can learn from each other by working together in small groups, so it would be rather odd if teachers could not.

Individual progress in a heterogeneous class

Discussions at the Seminar of workshop methods and team teaching had a vital effect in modifying our view of the major issue originally phrased as "One Road or Many?" Certainly while class teaching, examinations and externally imposed curricula persist, teachers of English will still have the task of deciding which pupils can be "entered" for a particular course and which cannot. Equally inevitably there will be sheep and goats, gilt letters on the notice-board for some, and graffiti on lavatory walls from others. But members of the Seminar, whether from the U.S., Canada, or Britain, found themselves repelled by the process of "streaming" or "tracking" (as it is generally known in the U.S.). "It was not streaming alone, or even primarily, that was opposed; our concern was rather with the whole complex of arrangements in selecting, sometimes as early as eleven, a number of children for an academic pattern of education while the others, not necessarily the weakest, receive a different and usually inferior type of education and are doomed to failure in advance. With such selection and rejection there tends to go an excessive concern for external examinations and the cramming necessary to pass these and qualify for the next stage. In England and Wales, streaming has been the official policy for some years, but this policy has recently begun to be reversed; in the U.S. the schools offer what is nominally the same education for all, but in fact much 'tracking', open or concealed, may be found from the beginning of the elementary school; in Canada tracking is on the increase."

There are particular reasons why teachers of English feel concerned about the problems they face when a school is streamed. When language is used for interaction in talk and drama, it is essential for a class to have a wide range of experience and background. Of course, if a social group becomes segregated, whether in predominantly Negro schools in the U.S., or in the predominantly working class C streams of the U.K., it will inevitably retreat into its own sub-culture and dialect, and the difficulties of encouraging a broader cultural awareness will become highly intractable. So much is obvious. What is less often recognized is the lack of concreteness, vitality and richness in the oral language of some upper stream pupils when they too, in their way, have been segregated. In the classrooms we have described, pupils from various backgrounds stand to gain from each other. Moreover, the process of streaming affects not only the pupils but their relationship with the teacher. The sense that work is being valued not in terms of personal growth but as evidence for or against a decision on streaming easily produces an atmosphere of anxiety, the pursuit of marks, and—for many—a sense of failure. The mutual trust on which an English teacher must build is rarely

achieved or kept, if these pressures are felt. Once again this affects
the whole quality of language in class, particularly for those in the
lowest streams. Thus David Holbrook's testimony:

"I found in teaching 'bottom stream' children that the effect on them
of having been placed in low classes all the way through school life was
depressing—in the psychological sense of feeling that the world was too
much against them, and that they did not have the resources to deal with it;
that they were not good enough; that the world was not benign. It was
harder for them to persuade themselves, or for them to discover, that they
were whole and good . . . I came to feel that if our society treats a quarter
of its children like this, then there is something gravely wrong with
prevalent attitudes to human beings."

A good deal of evidence suggests that any possible good influence
of academic sorting (streaming, grouping or tracking) upon the
work even of the abler pupils is only marginal; its influence upon
the work of the large middle range of pupils is bad. The learning of
prepared answers, the lessening of real personal interest, the lowering
of the standard which pupils set before themselves, and the lack of
concern for English for its own sake, all these are among the symp-
toms. "But it is the *social* effect of dividing children at an early age
into academic and non-academic 'streams', and in the U.S. into
corresponding 'tracks' which has been so particularly harmful for
education and English alike—particularly in the British conditions
of a severe shortage of places for the more academic kinds of secondary and higher education. The premature sense of failure in a divisive
school can only prepare pupils for a divided society.

To all this we opposed the unstreamed or unsorted school.
On social and humanitarian grounds it is clearly necessary. The
issue that has divided teachers in the past is whether it is educationally
possible: in a *class* of heterogeneous attainment would not the
weakest go to the wall—or the brightest suffer? So long as the discussion is in terms of *class teaching* of 30–40 pupils it seems inevitable
that the answer to this question must be, Yes. But it was widely felt
at the Seminar that class teaching inevitably limits what can be
achieved in English, however homogeneous the group is supposed to
be. Without a good deal of individual study, work in small groups,
assignments and project work, as well as work for part of the time
with the whole class, no pupil will attain that individual growth in

language which is basic to his progress in other subjects and his capacity to live fully and actively in society. When a pupil works in this way in English, gradually learning to take his part in the decision what to work at, the limit is indeed set by his brightness, independence and originality. Under the streamed system, with the class teaching it favours and even condones, much originality and independence never emerges and even the brightest pupil has to follow the routine of tasks set for the class. Moreover, in our subject the terms of the argument need scrutinizing: the facts are that creativity and imagination are not the exclusive province of academically bright children and young people. Indeed, among the Seminar reports it was noted that some of those destined early for an academic style of life developed such rigid intellectual controls as to become "emotionally disadvantaged", unable to respond fully to literature or life. Thus in response to literature, in drama, and in discussion and writing from personal experience, pupils of very diverse I.Q. score and social status can find they have something to learn from each other.

Conditions and pressures to be overcome

Nevertheless, "for a long time to come it will be difficult to achieve a school system without streaming"; in particular the English teacher will find it difficult to overcome the widespread environmental and administrative conditions that make for the practice.

The first task is to try to reverse the consequences of adverse conditions that may have built up during the first few years of a child's life, including the first year or two at school: "it may be almost impossible to overcome these consequences at a later stage. The pre-schooling period, as well as the early years at school, is therefore vital and the most certain guaranteee of solid progress, in academic work not less than in social development, will be a major effort beginning in the early years and continuing subsequently, to avert the difficulties before they happen or put to right the disadvantages at an early stage. Good practice in English must begin at the beginning and be built up gradually."

As a second stage of encouraging better practice, conditions in the schools themselves must be improved. Teachers in bad school buildings, with insufficient books and equipment, and a different set of

35 pupils to meet six or seven times a day, will have to be unusually capable and courageous to carry through a workshop approach. Even when these drawbacks are removed, something more positive will be needed. The pressures in the schools ought to be strongly educational, not anti-educational as with many examinations in English, or ambiguous and lukewarm as with the resultant syllabuses and curriculum guides.

However, the schools themselves are not free agents, and a third problem emerges. In the later years at school a new pressure develops, coming from the colleges and universities. "At the present time in all our countries the objectives of university-bound pupils are different from those of the rest. For them, objectives are conceived so much in terms of ground to be covered, examinations to be passed, and standards of proficiency to be reached, that English—for potential English specialists [majors] and others alike—too often becomes a means to an end." Some of this pressure, one suspects, is unnecessary and results from "the self-imposed isolation of the English professor from the teaching of his subject in the schools" to which Albert Kitzhaber self-deprecatingly referred. But a major issue may well remain: if the universities are genuinely unable to operate unless entrants have a specialist background already formed, and cannot accept in lieu people with mature experience of independent work [over a broader field], then the issue of One Road or Many genuinely emerges at sixteen. But one also hears university men say, in effect, "Don't do any of our work before you come up; we don't mind if you are taking History, we will still make you into ——."

There were thus three major questions facing the many advocates at the Seminar of unstreamed or unsorted schools. First, what could be done to minimize or eliminate the effects in school of poverty in the roles and language some young children learn at home? Second, given that an unstreamed, workshop approach to English had been developed with outstanding success in certain primary schools, how far could it be extended by specialist teachers of pupils eleven to eighteen? Third, how far did the demand or need for differentiation into specialist work preclude unstreamed classes beyond a certain age?

In a school system that accepts streaming these questions may never arise. When they are genuinely faced, given the conditions that most schools have to work in today, the response is generally to attempt work in unstreamed classes for part of the week, and for the remaining part to allocate pupils to "sets" or "groups". Such "setting" allows pupils taking the same *subject* to be grouped according to their current attainment, and may also allow pupils to select from a range of specialist options in one or more subjects. In schools working this system the subject department can have a voice in deciding whether classes for English, say, should be unstreamed or setted. Setting also permits college- or university-bound students to have times each week when from a range of options they can choose work directed to specific faculty requirements. The system is flexible; answers can range from almost complete setting to almost complete unstreaming. This is both its strength and its weakness: a dynamic school can move progressively away from streaming and setting, but many others will be content with static, "compromise" answers to the major questions. Thus the opportunity to seek a fundamental answer to the issues involved is easily pushed into the far distant future.

A proposal for international experiment

In the view of the Seminar a serious answer to the three major questions cannot be postponed indefinitely. Without a rigorous and concerted effort the existing problems of divided schools in a divided society will not be solved. On the diagnosis outlined here, the weakness is serious, a cure urgent. Individual schools can only take this so far; co-operation with universities and institutes of education is essential. We therefore recommend as a matter of urgency that an international experiment be carried out over several years in one or more districts of the U.S., Canada, and Britain, in which a group of schools, using buildings designed for the purpose, develop and extend new approaches to English of the kind we have proposed, in concert with analogous approaches now being pioneered in other subjects. (The concentration on new subject approaches would distinguish it from the not dissimilar eight-year study conducted by the Progressive Education Association in the U.S. before World War Two.) These schools would not introduce streaming or tracking between the ages of five and eighteen: pupils entering them would not take external examinations. Special arrangements would need to be reached with those universities that took part in the experiment so that pupils could be admitted on the basis of joint school-university consultation. Progress would be carefully followed.

Such an experiment would require a good deal of support and finance. It would be necessary first to ensure adequate, though not untypically good, buildings and material provision (including books); the teacher load would need to be kept down to a reasonable figure; a good deal of preparation, in-service education, recording and follow-up would be essential. The result would give some idea of what might be expected of normal students under reasonable conditions—conditions that, sooner than we think, economic development may make available to all.

Chapter 8

Teacher education

THE findings of the Seminar have broad implications first for initial education of teachers, in colleges and universities, and secondly for continuing education throughout their service. At both levels we foresee the need for profound changes.

At present, college and university education in both countries, diverse as the systems are, is creating barriers to the teaching of English as envisaged in this report. Clearly students who intend to teach the subject need wide experience in drama, and particularly improvised drama; continuing experience and encouragement in imaginative writing; and a confident grounding in the purposive talk that arises from group learning in an English workshop.

We seriously doubt whether more than a minority of teachers in training approach English in this way. Instead it often appears that the demand for intellectual rigour is so interpreted that it obscures rather than illuminates the process of using language to gain insight into experience at large. Our first concern therefore is that teachers of English at all levels should have more opportunities to enjoy and refresh themselves in their subject, using language in operation for all its central purposes—in imaginative drama, writing and speech, as well as the response to literature. Teachers without this experience—who would never think of writing a poem, flinch at the idea of "acting", and rarely enter into discussion of the profounder human issues in everyday experience—are themselves deprived and are likely in turn to limit the experience of their pupils. On the other hand, we were agreed that, just because language is so vital and pervading a concern, mature men and women can surprise themselves by the imaginative power they suddenly realize they possess, given the right opportunity.

Such activities offer more than an intellectual challenge. Like the best reading and teaching and discussion of literature, they are "bound to be processes of self-testing and self-exposure". The value of intellectual rigour, on the other hand, arises not from its imposition in the form of critical superstructure on a work of literature, but from its growth in a searching awareness of the complexity of language in operation.

We do foresee a much more intellectually demanding study of language among all teachers. Whatever their subject, they need an objective view of their own language and of that used by others. They need help in realizing the full importance of language in society and in the development of an individual's personality and view of reality. This is the kind of relevance language study can have for all intending and practising teachers. But it should equally be emphasized that in many areas of language there is every reason for a tentative, exploratory approach. Thus a new attention is being paid at present to the study of specialized varieties of English. But as John Sinclair remarked, "The linguistic theories have not yet caught up with the needs of teachers because of the present speed of change." All the more reason, then, for study to begin from an active investigation of language in adult life and among children and young people, as they learn to use language to cope with new roles and situations. There is every danger, in the old lecture approach, of "feeding in knowledge". An integration of theory and practice is called for if the study of language is to have any relevance to teaching. Field study and practical investigations must permit the close observation, and raise the questions and tentative hypotheses, that can then be dealt with in theoretical lecture discussions and seminars. Here, as elsewhere, experimental schools attached to colleges, television classrooms, and film and video-tape of students at work are likely to become prerequisites.

Studies at the linguistic level will need to link and cross-fertilize with other developmental studies (as suggested in Chapter 5). Preparation for teaching necessarily involves a careful study of the world of children and young people. This starts and has its roots in a student teacher's personal knowledge of small groups of pupils, in school and outside. Observing and working with such groups enables a student to integrate and test against experience the relevance of a wide range of studies: studies of pupils' talk, drama and writing and the worlds they embody; of works of literature that offer new insights into their lives; of psychological investigations; and of the ways children respond to their social environment. It is such studies, continued among practising teachers, that offer the basis of knowledge and awareness on which the day-to-day improvisations in English lessons can be firmly built.

At any time, continuing or "in-service" education should be a normal part of a teacher's work, we believe; in an era of change like the present there is a double need for discussion, continuing education, and curriculum development work. So far as teachers of English are concerned, we envisage this at three levels. First, classroom visits, discussions and department conferences in the one school, or with one or two like-minded neighbours. Second, local centre work (in English workshops) to exchange ideas, develop new approaches and materials, and evaluate them jointly with visiting teachers. Third (and not least) restocking and refreshing through experience in creative writing, drama, and study of literature; through seminar study of new research evidence on the language processes in general; and through discussion of new organizational developments. Such courses would involve bringing together teachers from schools, colleges and universities, a process in which the professional associations of teachers of English can be particularly helpful.

Whatever the level, the comments of Paul Olsen on the work in the U.S. curriculum centres would probably hold good: "My feeling is that in so far as we've done anything good it's been in creating a kind of intellectual community among college people and school people, working together, trying to go through the great tradition to discover what might be relevant to the question, trying to rethink these things for ourselves, trying to create curricular materials in very small groups which work intensively, trying then to elaborate the relationships between these materials, and sending people back to their own schools. When they get back to their own schools, they themselves create similar kinds of study groups; ... *they create their own curricula.*" The advantage of an abstract structure to which the material related, Olsen continued, lay precisely in the questions it raised: first, Where am I going? and then, Am I sufficiently perceptive—do I even know enough—to use this material? Instead of sending out teachers who have been lectured to death, we need to create this kind of questioning, and an underlying sense of common ground and purpose between schools, colleges and universities.

The school itself must become a major partner in the professional education of the teacher (whether for initial or continuing education). The attachment of college staff to schools and school staff to college is one way of expressing this. Another is through the workshop or open classroom, and team teaching that draws in people from school and college. Current experiments in the closer working of school and college deserve careful study: we badly need to find the best ways of integrating professional education.

The problem of advanced studies in education and the need for inter-disciplinary teams has already been mentioned (in Chapter 2). Centres are needed where research that touches the schools can draw on teachers' interest, experience and insight, while developing the basis for a more critical conceptual awareness. Scholarship and practice are bound to stay poles apart when the two sides are not asked to work together. Thus in a concluding footnote, we deplore the present isolation of colleges of education in England and Wales both from the universities and from other professional colleges. Staff and students need the contact of specialists in other fields, and thus in the long term a position in multi-purpose institutions like the liberal arts colleges and universities.

Chapter 9

In the perspective of the Seventies

I WANT to be personal and to ask what has happened to change my teaching, and my perspective on what I'm doing, since Dartmouth and 1966. I suppose the major change, which I'm still immersed in, still struggling to clarify, is part of the spirit of the age. It's not confined to English teaching at all—that's just one microcosm of a far wider struggle. It's about teacher and learner, parent and child, manager and worker. About the dilemmas of coercive authority and inescapable subordination. In the last eight years social consciousness of these dilemmas has spread, in an uneasy awakening. Within the microcosm, in the teaching of English, they have suddenly become totally clear. Listening to myself and to others in discussion with students, I recognize again and again how prone the teacher is to use his language to dominate and constrict. Learners are born free, but are everywhere in chains: what sounded like a slogan has become an inescapable truth. If we doubt it we have only to tape-record any run-of-the-mill lesson. The facts are there.

By the second international seminar (York, 1971) there were other tapes available, which seemed to show that, given a chance to talk among themselves, pupils made unexpected progress. They talked in their own terms. And this threw into relief quite unsuspected processes of feeling and thought, which class discussion dominated by the teacher's language had obliterated. This polarity was about as far as we got then. So where did our roles as teachers lie? Teaching had become a dirty word.

York 1971 sent us away to think about the teacher as listener, about our responses to what pupils had to say, about the possibility of sharing the role of learner, about students' initiatives . . . and a lot more. Is the polarity real? I think probably not. But if not, we still needed its simplicity to challenge us. There were roles we had to abandon, and others we have to discover.

Without a secure role it's easy to make mistakes, and also to panic. Perhaps in 1974 it's not so surprising to notice many signs of confusion, uncertainty, cynicism, and dogmatism in teaching. These could be the expected products, within the microcosm, of the uneasy awakening. I don't see this as a reason for disillusion. The questioning of power and subordination in contemporary capitalism— or in so-called communism—is a running battle that I expect to reach beyond my own lifetime. What's hard to bear is the confusion inside ourselves. We're beginning to see how adults can learn from children, and maybe what kinds of social relationships would release fuller potentialities in the converse process. But the social models built into us, and within which we work, consistently pressurize and distort the effort to create such relationships. I would be glad if better teachers than me could chronicle that struggle with all the concreteness and objectivity it needs. It demands an effort of personal discipline (and release) that I have still not achieved.

What has heartened me over the last few years is not the hope that the running battle would soon be over, but the sense of gaining a new perspective on what we are trying to do. Dartmouth proposed a new interest in the learner, his development, and the processes of using language to learn. As you see, this is a narrower field than the one that emerged in York 1971. It invites us to focus on the learner in abstraction from his social relationship with the teacher. Still, if we can understand people, ourselves included, in the process of formulating new perceptions and ideas at different stages in their lives, then we have a new basis for changing our roles as teachers. I believe that, over the past year or two, ideas have come together in such a way as to transform my perceptions, first in learning and teaching English, and second, in talking, writing, and reading well beyond the boundaries of that subject.

A transformation in our understanding?

Looking back, I realize now that the main theme had already been stated before Dartmouth, in Denys Harding's exemplary title, "Experience into Words". Language is only one way of symbolizing experience, and compared with visual images it appears to be very indirect. So I suppose an elementary question for a teacher to ask would be: what processes of selection and organization are going on, and what constraints are inevitably imposed, when we try to get experience into words?

I've called this question elementary because I don't see how we can understand English teaching if we haven't an answer, But it has taken me eight years to formulate it in such a way that a *coherent* answer seems possible. Again, looking back to Dartmouth, I realize that two of the Americans I most admired were already obsessed with this theme. I couldn't understand then, though I think I begin to now, why we in the seminar were so unable to make practical application of their powerful suggestions.

Let us first consider choices and constraints within the language. Suppose that we take a party of primary children out to a station, an airport, a power station, a castle, the coast, the mountains, or whatever, and that later they each talk or write about their experience. If they have some freedom in choosing what they want to say, very likely we shall find some sharp contrasts in the way they handle the experience. The first question is, can we trace any of these contrasts to inevitable choices in the language? Let's look closely at the following two examples.

Look out its coming see the train run about saying ch ch ch all the time and its about to come again, this time it is saying c c c come a gen a gen a gen a gen.

Adrian

When we got to the station I got off and had a look a round and we went down the subway and there was two ways out and we went to another platform which the subway led to, and went across a foot bridge and the foot bridge felt as though it was going to fall and when we got to the other end we went to ask a driver and he showed us three brakes and one of them was the main brake and the other brake was the brake for when the other broke and the last one was the deadmans brake and then we had to go home and I saw bridges and roads and fences mines sacks houses and all the way there I saw lines and our train in which we went on was about a 5000′ long.

Stephen

The clue is, of course, that as we read Adrian's piece aloud we are involved in an immediate experience—"Look out it's coming"; as we read Stephen, we are handling with more detachment an experience in the past. The evidence for this lies in the key verbs:

it's coming	I got off
saying	had a look a round
this time it is saying	we went down the subway

And there are other, associated contrasts. The "characters" in Stephen's narrative—I, we, and the driver—are named and one of them is narrator. (The fact that "I" and "we" are named indirectly, of course, tells us something about Stephen's sense of the audience he is writing for—but more of that later.) In Adrian's piece the characters are not so much named as presented: ch ch ch, look out. ... The narrator (or should we say enactor?) is not at all detached, in fact he seems to merge into the "characters" he evokes. This time it is saying c c c come a gen a gen a gen a gen. Is this describing the engine approaching or describing *being* it? It's hard to distinguish.

It looks as though there is a fundamental choice here in what Jim Moffett calls the *level of abstraction* at which the experience is handled. And even from these simple examples, the choice seems to have profound effects on the processes that go on as these children get experience into words. It seems vital that we should know more about such effects, but before considering them, let's look for other contrasts. Virginia, one of the same group, ended her piece like this:

... In the toilets there was a foot pump and when you turned a knob and then press a button a tap runs and its like a little shower. In the buffet part of the tain there is a man selling sandwiches and things. In another part of the train there is a man cooking hot meals, in the part of the train where there are people eating there is tables with cups and saucers plates serviettes and table cloths on the tables. If you stand on the part of the train where one carriage joins another you get a very wobbly feeling.

                                                                Virginia

My intuition tells me this is a more abstract level still. But after the opening sentence the verbs look at first as though they are conjuring up an immediate experience: there is a man selling ... a man cookin. ... On reflection, though, I see two contrasts with the other pieces. First a certain point of view is made clear, mainly by the words "there is . . . there are": these indicate an impersonal detachment from the events in progress. Secondly, the events are not in sequence, in fact the order is spatial:

In the toilets	there was	a footpump
In the buffet part	there is	a man selling
In another part	there is	a man cooking
In the part . . . where . . .	there is	tables

It seems significant that these precise indications of place give structure to the extract I have focussed on. Virginia is not enacting her characters, nor is she narrating events as she observed them, though it's all based on recent observation. Rather, she seems to be regarding this train as a type: it's only a small step further to forget *the* train of yesterday and to write "In the buffet part of *a* train there is *a* man selling sandwiches and things". (Come to think of it, she has already abstracted from the *particular* man she saw, hasn't she?)

To sum up thus far: these seem to be the first three of a set of fundamental choices (enacting, narrating, typifying . . . etc.), choices in level of abstraction governed by the key verbs; and associated with them, but distinct, are further choices between what I'll call personal or more impersonal points of view. Possibly we could go a step further and indicate the choices in structuring principles—Virginia's spatial formers were one instance—used like Meccano to build these minor constructions of the reality they encountered. But I'll leave that to you, if you're interested, because a second question ought to be asked: what's the significance of making these choices?

I take it that intuitively we're sharply aware of the differences for these three children. But can we make such intuitions explicit and try to generalize on them? I asked a group of teachers if they would try this on some similar material; here is a compilation of their initial comments for us to reflect on.

Effects or tendencies—

of enacting: it's like a play, enacting what has happened, but turning it into an event happening as it it is spoken about. Flashes and images capture the immediacy of the experience more vividly; it's like living through what happened. It tends to appear less organized, with an impression of movement, sound and the speed with which things happen, one thing breaking in on another. It arouses sympathetic feelings, the emotive power of the language being stronger than the referential.

of narrating: written with hindsight, there is more thinking about the event. It is easier to follow as a sequence: the account is ordered, giving detail, but trying to keep a smooth narrative. It is one person's view—all the experience seems modified by the writer, so that we are aware of seeing things through his eyes. Things are described from a distance in a calmer, less involved, more dispassionate way. It tends to a more explicit and complete account, with indications of a feeling for the reader.

These comments help me to see that any formal difference (in tense etc.) is interesting as a clue to deeper purposes in the writer. Conceivably, by a *tour de force*, we could reverse the purpose and still keep the same tense—I'm not interested in making hard and fast systems. But if as writers we follow the natural consequences of these choices in levels of abstraction, we seem likely to grapple with an experience in fairly distinct ways. To choose two phrases as a key: "living through" or "written with hindsight".

You don't have to be a teacher to know the range of motives that lead us to live through an experience again: from delight, from anxiety, from sense of shock, from grief, for reassurance, for pleasure, and, perhaps more deliberately, to understand, to expose ourselves to the actual. . . . This is why an appropriate response to Adrian is sympathetic delight in sharing his little shaping of the experience recaptured, perhaps joining in with him to extend and develop it together. For a young child, an outing into strange territory can be just such a flood of impressions as he re-enacts. I think this helps me to see the point of Stephen's looking "with hindsight". It could be quite an effort for him to see with detachment the flood of events; so he threads together the platform where they got off . . . the subway they went down with two ways out . . . the other platform the subway led to . . . the footbridge they crossed . . . and the driver at the end of it. He is not so much reliving as mapping. As he makes this map with hindsight, maybe, he records two other unforgettable things he learnt—the three brakes and their functions, and the tremendous length of the train. As it happens the contrast in mental process could hardly be sharper: Stephen's would be a very dull living through, and Adrian's a clueless mapping.

Without my exploring further the system of levels, these examples suggest two polar directions: moving down through the levels of abstraction, towards the enactive, we are likely to become more involved in an experience and can explore it personally from within, in all its particularity. Moving up in the levels, we gain more control, more intellectual grasp or comprehension. If we consider the ways we scan our everyday personal life, there's a constant tension between these two directions, I think.

I'd like to pause at this point, which is roughly equivalent to the kind of position Jim Moffett had reached in 1966, because I now realize how helpful his initial schema can be in defining the characteristic interests of my teaching of English. It reminds me that, in contrast with many other subjects, English is centrally concerned with the elementary levels of abstracting from experience, with enacting and narrating. It's true that intellectual maturity enables us to move on through generalization to theory, to organize wider fields of human experience in more abstract terms, and to engage in longer bouts of thinking at those levels. But English—and perhaps the Humanities?—ought to be a steady reminder that the need to grapple with experience through elementary levels of abstraction is not simply child's play, but a challenge for life. Literature should teach us, and our own writing help us to realize, the kind of imaginative effort and the care for language demanded if the narratives or enactments of personal experience are ever to be adequate. If these remain utterly crude, I don't see what use generalizations drawn from them can ever be. No amount of hindsight will help us to understand what we can't yet "live through".

Because of the prevailing academic tide it has to be pointed out that many generalizations in psychology, sociology, anthropology, history, and the like are abstracted from personal experiences, which are ordered at the lower levels of abstraction. If the historian's construction of personal experience, and the perceptions it incorporates, is crude, it is difficult to see how adequate generalizations can be formed. Equally, the testing of our generalizations about human living, and of our typification of people, occurs whenever we move into lower levels of abstraction. In this sense, both literature and the best discussion of experience that we achieve in English incorporate and test our abstracted arguments about vital issues—moral, social, and political.

Refining our polar models

I may have moved beyond Moffett's early position at this point, indeed I hope I have. At Dartmouth I shared his excitement in discovering a *system*—he had even found a paradigm based simply on the verb to happen: what's happening, what happened, what happens, and what may happen? I came to think of this as rather typically American: they tended to ask what a systematic analysis would look like, and turned to theoretical explanation at the higher levels of abstraction. The English, I felt, would tend to look for the roots of the system in actual instances. Perhaps I was wrong and it's more a matter of the stage one has reached in developing a theory? However, I wish I had thought then of trying to apply his abstract schema to empirical evidence; the refinements this leads to seem to me to double its explanatory power. I have time here only to consider one of these refinements.

Suppose that instead of looking at writing we turned to talk, to an extract from conversation between four girls of sixteen. What happens within the conversation to the level of abstraction? And what suggestive evidence of mental processes do we gain?

A: When we used to live in ... in Kennington ... they used to walk ... we used to walk across the bridge ... you know, walk round London ... used to be ever so happy and I can remember my parents walking along hand in hand ... you know ... giggling (Laughter) ... and there's me in between, you know, looking up ... and laughing our heads off we were ... and I can remember that clearly as anything. It's one of the first things I remembered ... you know, being very happy, just the three of us. Then the next thing I remember was me having to go away because my brother was born and he had pneumonia ... and he came along and it was horrible ... (Yes.) (Laughter). It splits up the family ... you know what I mean ... I was really jealous.
E: You were out of things ...

A: Yeah, I got really left out ... and it's been a bit like that ever since. I think that, like ... well, not only that—

B: I think parents begin to get out of touch with each other as husband and wife ... slightly, I should think ... I don't know ... it all depends what the couple's life's like ... er ... when they start having children. You see it takes so much of their time ... and it takes a certain place in their lives.

A: The husband gets left out a lot, doesn't he? (Yeah ... has a hard ...) (Laughter) ... No, you hear such a lot ... when perhaps ... when your dad come home in the evening and your mother will say, "Just a minute I'm getting so-and-so's tea ... Can you wait a bit?" ... You know, he's probably come home from work ... (Yeah).

B: Or, I've got my ironing ... or, I've got to take the children to bed ... and what not.

A: Yeah, I think that's when they get ...

D: My dad comes home and he sits down and says, "Will somebody get my slippers?" and nobody moves, you know ... Everyone's eating their dinner or staring at the television ... he feels very neglected I think ...

B: Probably because he feels everything should be done to him, you know (Yeah).

C: He's the father ... they should do everything for him ...

D: Probably been—

B: Head of the house ... as it were.

A: ... extra special attention ... which I think is right, you know ... I hope I remember that whenever I get married.

D: He's the one that goes out to work ... earns the money, as he says.

B: But then again, you find some families who ... don't take this attitude. They feel that ... both should be the sort of ... head ... you know ... eader.

I suppose the most striking thing is the way they shift from one level to another, within an utterance as well as between utterances. With a piece of writing it might be easy to imagine that the critical choice of level of abstraction is made once for all, or ought to be; here, in speech, I realize that a shift in level may also be significant. Consider A, for example:

> we used to live in Kennington
> we used to walk across the bridge, walk round London
>   used to be ever so happy
>   (I can remember)

```
    my parents walking along hand in hand, giggling
           there's me in between, looking up
                 laughing our heads off
              we were (I can remember that clearly as anything)
```

"Used to" makes the past actions recurrent, habitual and thus less particularized, as we can see. But as the memory arises, perhaps as a visual image, inviting "there's me", there is a sense of growing involvement with the experience, and the past incident slips momentarily into the present, thought it's a present regarded from a slightly detached point of view. "Then the next thing" introduces a skeletal narrative which rushes quickly on to the hindsight comment "It split up the family . . . I was really jealous".

If our friend makes an admission like that, what can be said in response? One possibility, as our sympathy carries us into the other's situation, is to try to turn the edge of guilt or regret, and to express our pity.

```
            A  I was really jealous . . .
            E  You were out of things . . .
            A  Yeah, I got really left out . . .
               and it's been a bit like that ever since.
```

After this second admission in an expressive voice, B chooses to respond in a different way:

```
          Parents begin to get out of touch with each other
          as husband and wife . . . slightly, I should think . . .
```

The effect, in this setting, is to generalize on A's plight, to place her feelings in the context of the whole family's, by implication, and to invite a more general concern for all parents, perhaps? What follows is a more detached, less egocentric, and less personally exposed discussion of the father's place; it is initiated by A as it happens, and carried by her and D back to the level of recurring and typical actions: "My dad comes home and he sits down and says. . . ." A slip into enacting is easily possible here.

There are more things you might like to study, especially the effect of B's concluding intervention. For the moment, I just want to consider the lessons I may have to learn from this tape. The first concerns the "choice" of level. I may seem to imply by this word that some deliberate selection takes place: in Adrian's or Stephen's case, I doubt if this is so. But somehow we "choose", inadvertently or not, one or other level of abstraction in much of the writing we do. Maybe what helps, what prompts us, is the previous rapid exploration of a whole variety of levels, precisely in conversations such as this. Thus, talk with shifting, undifferentiated levels of abstraction may form a natural prelude to any later choice of a differentiated level on which to explore further. If this is near the truth, I can see immediate implications for what I should be enabling as a teacher.

In fact, this example suggests to me that further exploration entirely at one level (in an autobiographical narrative, say), while it might deepen certain kinds of perception and understanding, might leave other things uncomprehended. This holds even more true of a dramatic re-enactment, I feel. And yet both these levels could offer significant opportunities for A to live through her past experience of happiness and jealousy, and to relate it more reflectively to the developing patterns of her family's life. It's just that *in this context* B's ability to generalize from the personal experience, to be aware of alternative perspectives, seems to be especially important too. Could we perhaps think of a conversation like theirs as a guide to the listening teacher, a series of suggestions for the many possible levels at which A or the others might want to pursue the underlying themes, possibly over a period of several days? If so, I think we should need E's tenderness and B's wisdom, as well as our own more abstract awareness of the processes going on, if we were to play an equally valuable role in talking over their work in progress and suggesting possible new perspectives.

This already revises my earlier view of teaching English, by emphasizing the value of verbalizing some of our deeper experiences at varying levels of abstraction, at times in search of fuller involvement with the dramatis personae, at times in search of greater comprehension and control. I take it that it's in these circumstances that one realizes the true value of generalization, as a valid way of expressing our fuller understanding of daily experience. I did not touch on this level of abstraction earlier, partly because it didn't arise in the primary children's writing. This is not to suggest, of course, that primary children don't generalize. But by sixteen or so, if teenagers get any encouragement, quite novel areas of experience may be reconstructed at this level, as part of a general movement away from childish egocentricity. I believe that in thinking of the role of father, and in considering the effects of parenthood on husband and wife, the girls are moving into an interesting border-land, on the edge of sociology and social psychology if they move in one direction, still in touch with narratives of personal experience if they move in the other.

Where on this border territory does an English teacher stand? There seem to be at least two schools of thought. The first I might call "literature-centred". It takes as its model the themes and the levels of abstraction characteristic of imaginative literature. At its most exclusive, this school sees itself as defending a tradition, with a dismissive wave to all else—"sociology". I think its great advantage lies in the clarity of focus offered to the young teacher. The second school I've called "experienced-centred"—perhaps a better term is needed. It shares the interest in a model based on imaginative literature, though it gives the primary emphasis to *pupils'* construc-tions of their personal and social worlds. When the borderland with sociology, psychology, history etc. is reached, teachers of this school venture in. The result is a much more diffuse range of studies, with dangers of confusion for the teacher. Their answer, I suppose, is that the borderland exists and *students'* confusion within it can't be overcome by fencing it round with subject specialisms. It was this territory, of course, that I explored with my friends Simon Clements and Leslie Stratta in our first book; so I was already aware of some of the issues in 1966. Why, then, you may ask, was this difference of emphasis between the two schools not raised at Dartmouth?

Some omitted questions

Every discussion has to start by taking some things for granted. When the participants bring with them the varying traditions of the United States, Canada and Britain, such things aren't always easy to find, which is part of the exercise, of course, but once found they tend to be grasped with satisfaction, and not submitted to further questioning. Looking back, one ought to be able to realize the common assumptions that were left unexamined, in the seminar and in this book, and to see how these focussed attention on some directions in English teaching, while neglecting others.

My own impression—and you are in a better position than I am to check this—is that the common ground we found lay in the teaching of imaginative literature, and this led I think to a common interest in its characteristic themes and levels of abstraction. (Actually there is strong circumstantial evidence to support this: someone counted thirteen pupils or colleagues of Dr. Leavis in the British contingent.) And Denys Harding himself, when he wrote "Experience into Words", was thinking mainly of the words we use in a certain kind of role: that of onlooker or spectator on experience. I feel the seminar made a vital contribution to our thinking about language and learning in the spectator role. What was left unexplored was the contrary role that he and James Britton drew our attention to (yes, even in the seminar)—the role of *participant*. This is their generic term for the roles we take on when we use language to inform, advise, convince, persuade, report, invite, order, request, instruct. . . .

It's a very large body of language to neglect. Such a thing couldn't have happened at Dartmouth if we had had a general theory of language functions as our common stock. Part of our advantage in 1975 is that the major lines of such a theory have now been proposed, by the Writing Research Unit at London. Although I won't attempt here to go into the details, what follows has obviously benefited from nine years of thinking and arguing with members of that Unit.

For the moment I'd like to focus on the participant choice in action. A Castleford boy went out with his junior class to a power station and in the course of the following few days wrote the piece below, under a drawing he had done.

First of all the coal comes down the river in the tom purkings barges. When it reaches the bank of the power station it is in nuts that is the little lumps of coal there is a conva belt waiting to take it to the grinding mills and then it is blown up a pipe to the bolers. The Grinding mills ground it into dust before it went up the pipe to the boiler. This is who it looks

Derek.

This is how it looks. The visual symbols in the drawing showed the objects in their spatial relationships. What do the verbal symbols add? They enable the writer to organize the key events into an ordered process, that's one thing.

> First . . . the coal comes down the river . . .
> . . . it is in nuts . . .
> There is a conveyor belt waiting to take it . . .
> . . . then it is blown up a pipe . . .

So far it seems to be simply a matter of rendering an experience into words. But in this example I think the young writer offers further clues as to what he is about.

> . . . it is in nuts, that is the little lumps of coal.
> . . . it is blown up a pipe to the boilers. (The grinding
> mills ground it into dust before it went up the pipe
> to the boiler.)

What is the significance of these additions? For me they mark the shift that occurs when we move on from organizing things for our own satisfaction only, to organizing them for others. This young writer is already realizing that "nuts"—a familiar enough word to him perhaps, brought up on the coalfield—may not be understood by everybody, and equally that those not in the know would need to be told explicitly that not nuts, but the ground dust, was blown up to the boilers (the accompanying change of tense is interesting). This kind of evidence suggests that as he writes he is beginning to imagine an audience other than himself and his classmates, and to take on the role of informing and explaining to that audience. If you remember Stephen's "we", a sign that the writer is still implicitly thinking of those who have shared the experience, you can imagine the demands made by Derek's step forward in the mastery of language.

Using language in a participant role implies that the perceptions, events, ideas, etc. are organized on behalf of, in the interests of, and for their effect on, another person or other people. Sometimes this second party is directly addressed, of course: "If you want to make some bubbles like we did, you have got to have some Fairy Liquid". In writing, though, this isn't always the case: there are simply clues in the organization that reveal we are implicitly seeking to instruct, convince, inform . . . *someone*. Can we generalize about kinds of clue, going beyond those we've already noticed? In general terms,

I suppose that in conjuring up an experience for ourselves, or for a close companion, we can take a great deal for granted (as A did when she recalled her memory). The effort to convince or inform someone who hasn't necessarily shared the experience, and doesn't necessarily share our assumptions, puts pressure on us therefore to be more explicit, to insert explanatory comments, to check for ambiguity, to be fuller in our descriptions, to take more care about making clear the organizing framework of our construct, to become aware of what we're assuming and to allow for alternatives—in short, to reconsider what we are saying from another, alien point of view.

Having said this, I'm reminded that the mastery demanded is never simply linguistic; it has psychological and social implications too. In fact, being able to use language in a participant role both follows from and enables a certain kind of social competence. Explanations, requests, directions, invitations, reports, instructions, advice, reminders, warnings—all verbalizations of this kind are a recurrent and necessary part of carrying on the business of our lives, in transactions with others.

Learning to master language in a participant role, then, implies learning to take on a wider range of tasks and responsibilities in a community. Or it ought to. I wonder how many schools today are encouraging *pupils* to give explanations, make requests, give directions, offer invitations, compile reports, give instructions, offer advice, send reminders, issue warnings . . . ? I don't mean in exercise books for the teacher to mark; I mean in fact. When you look back at the list don't you find these rather the prerogatives of the teacher?

Participant roles and the teacher of English

It seems, then, as though the teaching of English in participant roles may be much less understood than work in the spectator role with literature as our guide. Besides, it will be much more diffuse, for the kinds of transactions I have listed belong, or ought to belong, one would think, to lessons in any school subject. Perhaps the only sensible answer is the recent demand for a new language policy *across* the curriculum. But even if that is achieved, it still seems necessary to ask whether the teacher of English has anything to offer.

Let's consider the traditional answers first. I think they roughly imply that the teacher of English takes the main responsibility for:

(1) Mastery of writing as a medium:	handwriting, spelling, punctuation and "correctness" (Standard English grammar).
(2) Mastery of minimal "business" transactions:	letters of application, letters to the Press etc.; drafting and summarizing reports; précis; explaining technical processes; making accurate descriptions; etc.
(3) Mastery of reading for information:	"comprehension" questions.
(4) Mastery of informative and argumentative speech:	"lecturettes", debates, and more recently panels, forums, mock interviews, etc.

If we turn to the traditional textbooks of the 1950s some of the work on the right hand side was so ossified, so out of touch with actual learning and the real world, that it was tempting to write off the lot. Efforts to reform it in the 1960s (my own efforts included) just didn't go far enough in transforming the pupil's role in the school. However, if we look at the left hand side instead, it seems we shouldn't give up trying to find an adequate answer. What lessons can we draw from past mistakes? I'd like to propose three for consideration.

First, I don't think that language work in a participant role will succeed till it arises naturally in the course of bigger enterprises, organized with the class, or by groups of students; this applies in English as in other subjects. If this were established as a tradition, then simulation might become a real help, because it would be patently related to practice.

Secondly, given real audiences and readers, and something we want to say—feel glad to say, perhaps even feel we ought to—we are inevitably caught in responsibilities to our readers. If they are to be informed, advised, enlightened, apprised, . . . taught about something, we have to organize the verbal construct in its most effective form *from their point of view.* (I prefer to give this set of transactions priority, rather than repeat the dominant emphasis in our culture on the alternative set, where we wheedle, urge, indoctrinate, incite ... persuade in our *own* interests, or those of our clients.) How best can we organize our presentation, bulletin, magazine, forum etc. in the interests of the other party? The question already suggests the need for deliberation, for reflecting on each attempt, possibly for simulated experiment, and for revision. Derek is beginning to learn this. The comment of his that I put in brackets is retrospective: it can only arise from looking back to consider what more might need to be said, for the sake of someone less experienced in power stations. There are other problems for his readers that he hasn't yet realized, principally for any who don't know his dialect ("boler", "who it looks"). The teacher will decide on the best opportunity to discuss these.

The third lesson follows directly. Once deliberation begins, there is a developmental progression from particular, piece-meal insights into effective choice of language, to the generalized study of language in operation. At a later stage Derek might be interested to study some uses of dialect in his local community: the social occasions that bring it out at its broadest, for instance, the qualities it expresses, the ways in which it's modified in talk with "comers-in". By that time, if the school has given him adequate incentive to read, he'll have been equally exposed, roughly speaking, to the system of written forms (Standard English); this too will become an object of questioning and study, not as an abstracted system, but in operation. Since Dartmouth, the "Language in Use" materials produced by a Schools Council project team have suggested, far more concretely than the seminar was able to, what such studies could be like. These materials in turn have stimulated far more realistic discussion of "effectiveness for the reader". What they still await (and, I would guess, what will eventually transform them) is a reformed tradition of language work in participant roles. For, as often happens in our education system, we have asked for solutions at the more abstract levels (pupils generalizing and discussing theories) before finding them at the most concrete (pupils having the actual experience in school that calls for language in a participant role).

The first lesson would apply to all teachers, as I see it; the second

K

to all with a special concern for language as a means of expression and communication; and the third to teachers with a specialist interest in generalizing and theorizing about language in operation.

I must leave these particular suggestions for further discussion. But the underlying general point already corrects an imbalance in this book, I think. Its emphasis on language in the spectator role focusses our attention on "how we represent the world to ourselves, and ourselves to the world" (Britton). Our interest therefore is in the imaginative processes involved and in the adequacy of our language to represent experience(s). The central process is the act of *representing*. When we shift focus to include language in participant roles, the central process becomes the act of *communicating*. This is much more open to scrutiny and to public discussion, I would think, from its very nature. It's easier for others to point out to us where we have overlooked the needs of our audience, for instance, because in effect they can act as our audience! Thus in order to report, explain, advise etc. effectively, the written documents pupils publish for a wider audience have to be checked to see that there are no misleading ambiguities, and that idiosyncratic spelling or punctuation doesn't hold up the reader. The sources of information need to be carefully scrutinized, to make sure that what they intended to say has been accurately conveyed. If pupils want to convince real people, not the teacher in his role of marker, they may have to consider various ways of marshalling their arguments, and select the most telling points and illustrations.

I regret now that this side of English studies wasn't taken further in my report, or at Dartmouth. In part this has left the field open to recent unthinking claims that bookfuls of "exercises" in spelling, punctuation, "correctness", comprehension and précis, will somehow do the trick for this generation they failed to do for mine. In part it has held up serious discussion on more effective ways of helping pupils through various stages in the mastery of communication. If you don't believe that *every* spelling must be corrected, or that *no* correction is needed, then aren't you more obliged than usual to state your long-term strategy, and the grounds for it?

Equally important, I believe the implicit emphasis on the spectator role has tended to narrow the definition of literature. In a more restricted sense this means works of fiction—in poetic, dramatic, or prose narrative forms. These are the works which in the main (but not exclusively, as we'll see later) use the enactive and narrative levels of abstraction. But in the broader and more traditional sense, literature includes a variety of other work: Defoe's *Journal of the Plague Year*, an early form of documentary; Johnson's moral essays; Southey's *Life of Wesley*; Hazlitt's *The Spirit of the Age*; Orwell's *The Road to Wigan Pier*; Baldwin's *Notes of a Native Son*; Berger's *A Fortunate Man*; Blythe's *Akenfield*—I'm naming some past and present favourites and you'll think of others. If we take these as exemplars, they remind us that in the British literary tradition— and how much more the Classical or the French?—the imaginative writer has frequently been absorbed in more than fiction. Some of this work, I suppose, borders on History, Politics, Ethics, Sociology. Much of it reaches up from the elementary levels of abstraction into generalization. We are back in the borderland I mentioned earlier. What has changed its complexion for me is the realization that this involves a shift in the language used from a spectator towards a participant role.

I say "a shift . . . towards" advisedly. Reconsidering some of these works, I suspect there may be an ebb and flow between informative and artistic purposes. How far is it inevitable that we assimilate the story we tell to the mythic patterns we know—and how far are we tempted on occasion to see *this* man, *this* historical event we are describing, as in part symbolic of all men and all human events? These are fascinating questions which I must set aside for the moment, accepting the simple opposition between works that are spectator/participant because its crudity sharpens my awareness of important language processes I skated over in 1966.

The exemplary works I mentioned above, and others one might draw from film and television, suggest that some work in the participant role will be central to English. I've tried to make a list. The careful observation of people in action in their daily lives (Orwell); the reconstruction of key moments in their lives from statistics and documentary evidence (Defoe); the collection and editing of a faithful record of their personal histories, and the collective story of their local community (Blythe); the attempt to document and relate the significance of one individual's life story (Berger); the characterization of representative figures in our society (Hazlitt);

and reflections on the personal insights one gains from all such work —that would be my way of translating into broad classroom possibilities what I've learnt from the writers I named. I've no doubt the list could be added to, especially in the more generalized levels. What characterizes a list like that? It's still work that calls for imagination, I think. To give it a rough title, in opposition to Fiction I'd call it Documentary. This stresses the observing, recording and reporting that form the primary basis of the work, the prerequisite if the complementary part—the explaining, reminding, warning, and appealing to an audience in a participant role—is to be of any value to them or to the writer.

Expressive and communicative purposes

You may feel by now that I am pushing the contrast between participant and spectator roles a bit hard, and indeed I have been. To define work in participant roles as sharply as possible I have considered the struggles we get involved in when we try to inform, persuade, etc. an audience with *little* common experience and a rather *different* frame of assumptions. It's just such a party that we feel ourselves *able* to inform etc. about matters central to our experience and frame of reference. The Dereks have to realize that there are people actually ignorant about the operation of power stations. (That's why it's useless to ask such pupils to write for the teacher, who saw it all and possibly helped to explain it!) But of course there are things more personal than power stations to report, explain and convince people about; and for these we need an audience who have more in common with us, and are more like ourselves, perhaps. I wonder if this is where we return to the four girls talking? Somewhere along the gradient from "distant" to "intimate" audience, I fancy that our role ceases to be fully participant; it's less for others, more for ourselves, without caring much about the "effect", that we are verbalizing the experience. Already, in the case of levels of abstraction, a less clearly differentiated stage seemed to be of value in exploring a theme and making preliminary links between experiences. Perhaps a similar thing obtains in the case of spectator/participant roles?

In looking for an instance to discuss I've found the best field is the primary schools around me—a point to consider later. Here is a young junior school boy whose writing, I think, still relies for its effect on his spoken voice; you might like to try rendering it aloud.

Yesterday we went to Ann Louises farm it was very nice and we had some pop and finger (biscuits) after we had a ride on the pony it was a very nice pony but he kiked you and Mr. Cressey said do not go against his back legs so we did not go against his back legs we saw some cows and pigs and I loved everything the pig went puff puff and they snored and we all smiled Some cows were brown the cows hit hit the other cows with their tails it made everybody smile. I had some scathes on my legs when I got out of the farmyard I climed a tree Martin climed to the top of a tree he climed on the branches how lovely it was to go on a farm I liked every bit of it and some cows dansted around the farm it was funny we all smiled becors it was so funny we ran a(nd) fell but we got up and ran away and we had to make a house for Mr. Cressey he showed us how to way the milke he said tomorrow a lorry will come and take the big cans to the dairy and put it and put it in a bottle and put red or silver milk tops Steven Jons was the first to have a ride on the pony and he fell off the pony he smiled and everybody else smiled to it was half past three we had an hour to see the pigs and we saw the pig and Mr. Cressey put the lights on and so we could see the pigs it was nice to ride on the bus we had to pay 2d and we broght 4p for coming back and the cows went moo-oo we all saw the hens and one cow went mad we all ran about and jumped about. we climed tree and climed huts it was lovely we ran past (tractors) evry body fell on the floor you could go on a rocking hores we picked sticks we danst about we shouted at the cows one cow ran round 8 time I thort it had gone crazy it was black and brwon and some was white anothey was all corles. We went in the garden to play when we were coming home we came down the hilly fields so we could a run and we saw a fire it was red and yellow we saw them milking the cows with a mersheen they tied the cows with chanes how lovely it was but it smeled horidle they had big bucets to put milk in and then they waied the milk to see how mutch the cow had then they put it in to a book so they could see how mutch the cow had they showed the teachers the record book and one cow was called Louise it is a lovely name for a cow everybody else thought it was a lovely name. I saw the hens so did Garry Thickbroom so did Carol Upstone everybody saw the hens they were brown like a cow and the teacher said now it is time to go home and we said to Mr. Cressey thanck you for taking us round the farm.

Michael.

When I first read this to a group, the whole experience seemed to come pell-mell at me, like a kaleidoscopic sequence of images, all imbued with the excitement and pleasure of the writer. As one student said, it speaks as much about Michael as about the farm; in fact I suppose I can't really dissociate the two. Perhaps this was the most significant of our first impressions. Later, we realized that at two points at least there were passages with a sort of inner unity. The first and more obvious started from "we saw them milking the cows with a mersheen", (line 28). They tied the cows with chains . . . had big buckets to put the milk in . . . then they weighed the milk to see how much . . . then they put it in a book. . . . In this passage we seem to come down to severe practicality, though a tone of wonder and admiration might still be appropriate. Events are got into order, much in the manner of Stephen, or even Derek (thinking of the aside "so they could see"). True, there's a personal interjection: "how lovely it was but it smeled horidle". Still, the move towards a participant role, an informative function, seems clear enough. The second passage struck us after several readings: it starts from "and one cow went mad" (line 20) and seems to end several lines later. We all ran about . . . jumped . . . climbed trees . . . climbed huts . . . ran past tractors . . . fell on the floor . . . picked sticks . . . danced around . . . shouted . . . and one cow ran around eight times . . . I thought it had gone crazy. All these actions are thrown together in their own kind of dance till, with a build-up to the climax, we get the final comment. The rhythm, we thought, enacts the experience and is shaped by the impulsive excitement. In fact, it's like an embryonic poem: so we thought of this as a movement in the opposite direction, towards a spectator role. Thus the whole piece suggests a construction of the experience from which either role might develop.

Recently I have looked more closely at its entire organization with a group of teachers. We finished rather daunted by the evidence of very clear structuring that emerged: in verbalizing, the human brain seems to move towards a simple system, however free the surface looks. What struck us most, though, was the importance of the refrain that runs through the piece:

> it was very nice
> and I loved everything
> and we all smiled

it made everybody smile
how lovely it was
I like every bit of it . . .
it was a lovely name
thank you for taking us round the farm

It's like a theme and variations. That seemed in some ways a key to the way the experience was being operated on, as the young writer verbalized it.

On reflection, this piece and others like it bring out a fundamental contrast in language, I believe. I have used "communication" to indicate the way we organize language for others. What about the other pole, when we organize language for our own sakes? At that pole, instead of considering the effect of our feelings and attitudes on others, we just let them loose. Instead of having to take care that everything's clearly ordered, we can switch back and forward on impulse, to suit ourselves. There's no need to be explicit because we know what we're talking about. If we call this "(self-)expression", we are in a position to explain that initial feeling that the piece tells as much about Michael as about the farm. It's not "pure" expression, if that's conceivable anyway, beyond an exclamation or a curse. The piece has a sense of audience, though quite an intimate one, I would say. And the two major roles—spectator and participant—do seem to emerge in turn, each constructed with specific organizing units or "members". But the theme and variations, which give a kind of unity to the whole piece, both *state* and *express* something of its underlying intentions.

The London Writing Unit first awoke me to what was going on in such a piece. Using a convenient term, they have called its function "expressive". This is fine, so long as it doesn't obscure their main point: that precisely because it's undifferentiated, there's *an ebb and flow* between two poles, communication and self-expression; that there's room for a more differentiated role to emerge for a time, but that the *overall* organization is neither on spectator nor participant lines; that the audience is felt to be in on most of the experience, but not on all of it. I would prefer to keep the word "expressive", for the moment, to indicate a pole towards which the speaker/writer may tend, or, to shift the metaphor, a weighting he may give to one of the two potentials that run through language.

What purposes are served when writing moves towards the expressive pole?—this seems the most important question for us to ask as teachers. I think the main clue lies in the writer's release from the *demands* of an audience, and his sense rather of their *support*. This is exactly the feeling I get from listening to the tape of the four girls talking, too. If the audience is prepared sympathetically to follow the speaker/writer wherever the spirit takes him, if he is released from obligations to others, he is free to follow his own impulses, and the shifting directions in which these send the stream of impressions, images, perceptions, ideas. . . . It's a situation close to play and exactly similar to that of Stephen on page 24. When the experiences or ideas are deeply absorbing, the sense of an audience can encourage us to take verbalizing further than we anticipated, to realize new possibilities in it perhaps—but not to *explain* them yet, not to have to work to carry them through with a clearly differentiated function.

This is probably the most original discovery since Dartmouth. Unless one knows about the possibilities, such writing could easily be disregarded or pre-empted. It probably is, in most secondary schools now. I don't think this is because we grow out of the need for it, or because the personal springs for it dry up entirely after childhood. In fact, in the series of seminars from which I learnt most last year, I came to expect a break towards the expressive in the course of the first hour and a half, and to see it as the prelude to a concluding rally to new perceptions and a constructive reorganization of our ideas. In adult writing, the best examples I know to illustrate such processes come, not surprisingly, in letters to close friends (especially in Keats) or intimate journals (Dorothy Wordsworth's).

May 16th 1800. Friday morning. Warm and mild, after a fine night of rain. Transplanted radishes after breakfast, walked to Mr. Gell's with the books, gathered mosses and plants. The woods extremely beautiful with all autumnal variety and softness. I carried a basket for mosses, and gathered some wild plants. Oh! that we had a book of botany. All flowers now are gay and deliciously sweet. The primrose still pre-eminent among the later flowers of the spring. Foxgloves very tall, with their heads budding. I went forward round the lake at the foot of Laughrigg Fell. I was much amused with the business of a pair of stone-chats; their restless voices as they skimmed along the water following each other, their shadows under them, and their returning back to the stones on the shore, chirping with the same unwearied voice. Could not cross the water, so I went round by the stepping-stones. The morning clear but cloudy, that is the hills were not overhung by mists. After dinner Aggie weeded onions and carrots. I helped for a little—wrote to Mary Hutchinson—washed my head—worked. After tea went to Ambleside—a pleasant cool but not cold evening. Rydal was very beautiful, with spear-shaped streaks of polished steel. No letters!—only one newspaper. I returned by Clappersgate. Grasmere was very solemn in the last glimpse of twilight; it calls home the heart to quietness. I had been very melancholy in my walk back. I had many of my saddest thoughts, and I could not keep the tears within me. But when I came to Grasmere, I felt that it did me good. I finished my letter to M.H. Ate hasty pudding and went to bed... ... Going out in the morning I met a half crazy old man. He shewed a pin cushion and begged a pin, afterwards a half-penny. He began in a kind of indistinct voice in this manner: "Matthew Jobson's lost a cow. Tom Nichol has two good horses strayed. Jim Jones's cow's broken her horn, etc. etc." He went into Aggy's and persuaded her to give him some whey, and let him boil some porridge. She declares he ate two quarts.

It calls home the heart. ... Maybe whenever an experience is deeply moving and personal, we are glad to have some medium to express our response—music, movement, images, or language. And a phase where we are free to follow the ebb and flow between expressive and communicative impulses may then become the natural precursor to more careful, deliberate learning, when we are ready to meet the demands of an audience. It seems that we teachers shall only establish whether this is so by trying it in our practice.

The place where it's most needed today, I would suggest, is in response to the experience of literature. I say this after reading over the past three years a sample of A-level examination scripts (written by a selective group of 17 to 18 year olds). The joylessness of so much of the writing becomes actually painful after a time. I know the poor devils have an eye on the clock, and the tone of the questions is sometimes routine hack, but even when the examiners do their best to encourage a personal felt, comment they rarely meet with a response. This isn't simply a British phenomenon, either; at the York 1971 seminar there were similar accounts from the States and Canada, despite the different exam structures. The only conclusion we could draw there is that writing towards the expressive pole is either never encouraged or actively inhibited as "academic" education for the young adult begins to make its full demands. And looking back at my own practice, I can see the constraints I unthinkingly imposed or accepted in written work with this age group.

A teacher's agenda

There will be other lessons to learn, and some may already have occurred to you: this postscript is intended to be an essay to stimulate further thinking and discussion, not a fully developed statement. Nevertheless, I'd like to turn back and sum up reflectively what the last nine years have helped me to realize about teaching and learning English, and the agenda that this has set me personally.

What I have been tracing, I suppose, are two processes of differentiation. First, differentiation leading to a specific level of abstraction. I now want to sharpen my awareness of the "choices" that students and I are making, in ignorance or by intuition. I want to remove unnecessary constraints on the level of abstraction, particularly the ones I have been responsible for as teacher, and to learn in practice when it's helpful to suggest or propose one level of abstraction rather than another—and when it's best to leave them undifferentiated.

Second, differentiation leading to a specific communicative role: I need to find many more ways of encouraging that fruitful play with experience and ideas that can emerge when talking and writing move freely between expressive and communicative poles. (This will particularly affect my work in literature.) I want to be more perceptive about the embryonic poems, explanations, etc. that students and I incidentally produce and may want to develop later on, because the experience and ideas have involved us so fully.

Within language in participant roles, I'm sure I could make better use in the classroom of what I've learnt from Hazlitt, Orwell, and the rest. A wider range of classroom work in documentary needs to be published and discussed, alongside and perhaps related to work in fiction. (The secondary schools in particular don't seem to have exploited this opportunity to anything like the extent of the West Riding primary schools I've freely drawn on here.)

If I can work *with* students, sharing the responsibility for planning our joint enterprises—acting as chairman, secretary, or consultant—the transactions they get involved in will offer them new opportunities to master a wide range of participant roles. Then there should be room for me to act as a sympathetic and a critical audience, as the need arises. This means thinking again about the best ways of broadening and generalizing on insights into "effectiveness for reader" as well as "value for self".

It seems a big job! If it didn't, there would be no point in writing this, and attempting to involve other people in it. No point in making such a meal of theorizing, either. All that I have seen of continuing teacher education since Dartmouth—working with friends in Canada, the U.S. and Australia, as well as in Britain—has strengthened my belief in the potentialities of groups of teachers, providing they can find effective ways of working together. In so far as I've really been able to make this essay serve such groups, I'll be satisfied.

This isn't the end either. I wanted to fit in a section moving on from Paul Olson's interest in the myths by which we and our students live, and drawing in poetic symbolism. But the ideas are still too fragmented for me to synthesize in the space that's left. So, for me at any rate, there are further steps in theoretical analysis to be mastered.

Sources of Pupils' Writing

45 and 46   Sybil Marshall's presentation to the Seminar.

48, 50 and   Material presented by Connie Rosen.
   55

24, 26,   Conference reports of the London Association for the Teaching
   30 and   of English, and their anthology "And when we were young."
   53

7   Jane Westlake and Diane Wright.

63   Bernard Newsom of the London Institute of Education.

68 and 69   Simon Clements of Kingsway Day College, London.

4   *English in Education*, ed. Jackson and Thompson (Chatto).

49   *The Excitement of Writing*, ed. Clegg (Chatto).

113–14   Jean Frogget and Rosemary Finn, Bretton Diploma Course, 1972.

118–19   *Language, the Learner and the School*, Barnes, Britton and Rosen (Penguin 1969).
   Copyright © Douglas Barnes, James Britton, Harold Rosen, and the London Association for the Teaching of English, 1969

123   Mavis Turner, Primary Adviser, Wakefield Metropolitan District.

I should like to thank all those who made this material available and acknowledged with thanks permission from the copyright holders for previously published extracts.